FARMHOUSE
COOKING

*Traditional and Contemporary Meals
From Our Country Kitchens*

KATHY BLAKE

TODTRI

This book was designed and produced by Todtri Productions Limited
P.O. Box 572,
New York, NY 10116–0572
FAX: (212) 695-6984

Printed and bound in Korea

ISBN 1–880908–41–7

Author: Kathy Blake

Publisher: Robert Tod
Book Designer: Mark Weinberg
Production Coordinator: Heather Weigel
Senior Editor: Edward Douglas
Project Editor: Cynthia Sternau
Associate Editor: Linda Greer
Assistant Editor: Don Kennison
Picture Reseacher: Ede Rothaus
Typesetting: Command–O, NYC

PHOTO CREDITS

Charles Braswell, Jr. 78

Bullaty Lomeo 24–25, 76–77, 78–79

Sonja Bullaty 4–5, 8–9, 17, 69, 120–121, 143

Richard Day 110–111, 136–137

Dembinsky Photo Associates
Willard Clay 6–7
M.L. Dembinsky, Jr. 28
Darrell Guline 22
Adam Jones 39

Envision
Ed Bishop 23
Dennis Galante 38, 71, 82–83, 130–131
Peter Johansky 124–125
George Mattei 40–41, 44–45, 65
Rudy Muller 36–37, 135
Steven Mark Needham 10, 12, 13, 14, 18, 20–21, 26–27, 29, 30–31, 32–33, 34, 43, 46, 47, 48–49, 50, 51,
52–53, 60, 62–63, 66, 68, 70, 74, 75, 79, 80, 84–85, 86, 87, 90–91, 92, 93, 94–95, 97, 99, 100, 101, 102, 103,
106, 107, 108–109, 112, 114, 115, 117, 122, 123, 126, 127, 128, 129, 132, 133, 134, 138, 139, 140–141
Osentoski & Zoda 64, 81
Pictures of London 16, 61, 118–119
Amy Reichman 54–55, 96
Stock Food 58–59

Karen Kent 56–57

Angelo Lomeo 72–73, 104–105

Nawrocki Stock Photo 19, 142

Picture Perfect USA
Linda Burgess 67

CONTENTS

* *

INTRODUCTION

In these days of fast food, quick service, hurry-and-get-it-done, we can get quite nostalgic for times when life's pace was slower and quieter, when cooking and eating were group and family activities that served to nourish hearts and relationships as well as bodies. Farmhouse Cooking captures the atmosphere and remembrances of those times in recipes and photographs, and offers ways that today's busy cooks can create warm meals and memories for family and friends—whether they live on farms, in suburbs, or in cities.

Many suburban Americans today plant gardens, growing their own tomatoes, zucchini, cucumbers, fresh herbs, even corn and other crops, and derive great satisfaction from the process of planting, caretaking, harvesting, and finally enjoying the eating and sharing of the product of their labors. City dwellers who don't have the space for gardening continue to crave the incomparable taste and goodness of the fresh produce they remember from childhood. In many urban areas, farmers' markets abound, bringing a little farm life into the metropolis.

Of course, these days, with air-freight deliveries from any place in the world, our markets supply nearly any fresh fruit or vegetable year round. Huge produce departments in acres-wide supermarkets overflow with strawberries from Mexico, kiwifruit from New Zealand, grapes from Chile, pineapples from Puerto Rico, and apples from Australia. We don't have to wait for these products to be in season in our area any more, but when they are in season and locally grown they're less expensive and often tastier and fresher—worth waiting for.

As seasons change, the meals we plan and prepare change, too. Light entree salads, refreshing cold soups, and picnic foods fill the bill during the long days of the summer months. Winter's cold weather makes us crave hearty soups and stews, warm drinks, and hot, fresh breads.

In every part of the country, in every living situation, in every season, cooking and sharing food is an integral part of hospitality and celebration. Think of any occasion—birthdays, weddings, holidays—and there are particular foods we associate with each of them; in fact, many holidays were and still are referred to as "feast days." Traditional foods help us define and commemorate important events in our lives, and Farmhouse Cooking helps us remember and bring some of the good times from the past into our present.

CHAPTER ONE

SPRING FRESHNESS

From the moment the first warm breath of spring blows by, we begin thinking of enjoying the earliest crops of the season. Crunchy radishes, tender young lettuces, and asparagus stalks become available on the market or from our own gardens. Although many products that used to be obtainable only in the spring are now at the market all year round, we still honor the tradition of welcoming spring with meals that feature lamb or veal, new potatoes, and northeastern blueberries.

To get into the spirit of the season, try making some new springtime treats. Perfect additions to lunch or dinner, Asparagus Soup and Wild Thyme Asparagus are just two ways to satisfy the urge for those precious stalks. And when other irresistible produce appears, Watercress and Radish Salad, Red Potato Salad, and Blueberry Crumb Cake are creative alternatives for enjoying these gifts from the earth. And don't forget to take advantage of the year's first flowers. Place a big vase filled with colorful tulips or daffodils on the table to make any meal festive.

Spring also brings joyful holidays and opportunities to gather friends and family to share food and fun. On March 17, everybody—whether Irish by birth or not—can enjoy the "wearin' o' the green" and cook up a feast of Corned Beef and Cabbage or Irish-style Lamb and Potato-Dumpling Stew. A tart lemon pie, piled high with meringue, is a nice, light dessert for a special St. Patrick's Day meal.

Of course, Easter and Passover are the most joyous reminders that spring and life have returned to the earth, and every family has its own traditional foods that mark the occasion. If you'd like to try something new this year, consider the following menu: Deviled Eggs, Creamy Carrot Soup, Roast Stuffed Leg of Lamb, Mashed Potato Salad, Mixed Green Salad, and Bundt Cake with White Icing as a fine finish.

SALADS, STARTERS, AND SOUPS

WATERCRESS AND RADISH SALAD

juice of one lemon (about 2 tablespoons)
1 tablespoon honey
1/3 cup olive or vegetable oil
pinch salt
pinch pepper
1 large bunch watercress
3/4 cup red radishes, trimmed and thinly sliced
3/4 cup white radishes, trimmed and thinly sliced
1/2 cup chopped green pepper
6 large lettuce leaves

In a screw-top jar, shake together lemon juice, honey, oil, salt, and pepper until well blended; set aside. Rinse watercress and pull leaves from stems; discard stems. Just before serving, in a cold salad bowl toss together watercress, radishes, and green pepper; pour dressing over vegetables and toss well. Serve on lettuce leaves on cold salad plates. Makes 6 servings.

MIXED GREEN SALAD

1/2 cup mayonnaise
1/4 cup buttermilk or plain yogurt
2 tablespoons chopped chives
pinch salt
pinch pepper
6 cups loosely packed mixed salad greens, rinsed, dried, and chilled

In a small bowl, mix together mayonnaise, buttermilk or yogurt, chives, salt, and pepper; cover and refrigerate 2 hours. Just before serving, stir salad dressing, then toss salad greens with dressing in a cold salad bowl or arrange greens on individual plates and pass dressing. Makes 6 servings.

Mixed Green Salad

BLUE CHEESE DIP

1/2 cup mayonnaise
1/2 cup sour cream
3 ounces cream cheese
2 tablespoons sugar
2 teaspoons prepared mustard
1 clove garlic, finely chopped
4 ounces blue cheese, crumbled

Bring all ingredients to room temperature. In a bowl, beat together the mayonnaise, sour cream, cream cheese, sugar, mustard, and garlic until smooth; stir in blue cheese. Cover and chill until serving. Can also be used as a salad dressing. Makes about 1 1/2 cups.

BEER CHEESE SPREAD

1 pound sharp cheddar cheese, finely grated
2 tablespoons finely chopped yellow onion
2 tablespoons ketchup
1 teaspoon Worcestershire sauce
1/8 teaspoon red pepper sauce
1/3 cup beer

Bring all ingredients to room temperature. In a bowl, toss together the cheese, onion, ketchup, Worcestershire sauce, and red pepper sauce. Gradually mix in the beer, beating with an electric mixer until smooth and fluffy. Cover and chill until serving. Makes about 2 cups.

ASPARAGUS SOUP

1 pound asparagus, trimmed and cut into quarters
1/2 cup chopped onion
1 stalk celery, chopped
2 tablespoons butter or margarine
2 cups milk
1 teaspoon salt

In a large saucepan, bring asparagus, onion, celery, butter or margarine, and 1/2 cup water to a boil; reduce heat and simmer 20 minutes or until vegetables are soft. Cool slightly, then puree in a blender or food processor until almost smooth. Return vegetables to the pan; stir in milk and salt; heat but do not boil. Ladle into soup bowls and serve. Makes 4 to 6 servings.

Deviled Eggs

DEVILED EGGS

1 (2-ounce) can deviled ham

1/4 cup sour cream or plain yogurt

1 teaspoon prepared mustard

1/4 teaspoon salt

2 tablespoons minced celery

6 hard-boiled eggs, chilled, peeled, and
cut in half lengthwise

paprika for garnish

In a small bowl, mix together deviled ham, sour cream or yogurt, mustard, salt, and celery. Add cooked egg yolks and mash well. With a small spoon or a piping bag, fill egg whites with mixture, heaping well. Sprinkle each egg half with paprika. Chill well before serving and keep cold. Makes 6 servings.

CREAMY CARROT SOUP

8 medium carrots, peeled and cut into chunks

1 sweet potato, peeled and cut into chunks

1 large yellow onion, peeled and cut into eighths

2 cloves garlic

2 cups chicken broth or water

2 cups milk

6 tablespoons sour cream or plain yogurt

chopped parsley for garnish

In a large saucepan, bring carrots, sweet potato, onion, garlic, and broth or water to a boil. Reduce heat and simmer for 45 minutes, or until vegetables are very soft. Cool slightly, then puree in a blender or food processor until smooth. Return vegetables to the pan; stir in milk and heat but do not boil. Ladle into soup bowls and garnish each serving with a tablespoon of sour cream or yogurt and a sprinkling of parsley. Makes 6 servings.

Creamy Carrot Soup

MAIN DISHES

MACARONI AND CHEESE DELUXE

1/2 pound elbow macaroni
1/2 cup butter or margarine
1 cup chopped fresh mushrooms
1/2 cup chopped onion
1/2 cup chopped red bell pepper
1/2 cup chopped green bell pepper
1/4 cup flour
2 1/2 cups milk
1/2 teaspoon nutmeg
3 cups grated American or cheddar cheese

Heat oven to 350° F. Grease a 2-quart casserole dish; set aside. Prepare macaroni according to package directions; drain and set aside. Meanwhile, melt butter or margarine in a large saucepan; sauté mushrooms, onion, and red and green peppers until tender. Stir in flour and nutmeg; cook, stirring, until bubbly. Add milk all at once; stir until thickened and beginning to boil. Remove from heat and stir in 2 cups cheese until melted. Add cooked macaroni and pour into prepared casserole; sprinkle with remaining cheese. Bake 30 minutes, or until bubbly around the edges. Makes 6 servings.

SPAGHETTI PIE

1 1/2 cups milk
3 eggs
1 cup cottage cheese
3/4 teaspoon salt
2 cups cooked pasta (hot or cold)
1 cup red spaghetti sauce, such as marinara or meat sauce
1/2 cup finely grated Parmesan cheese

Heat oven to 375° F. Grease a 10-inch pie plate; set aside. In a bowl, stir together milk, eggs, cottage cheese, and salt; add pasta and spread in prepared pie plate. Top with sauce and sprinkle with Parmesan. Bake 30 minutes or until set. Cut into wedges to serve. Makes 6 servings.

Macaroni and Cheese Deluxe

LAMB AND POTATO-DUMPLING STEW

LAMB STEW:
3 tablespoons butter or margarine
3 onions, sliced into rings
1 teaspoon paprika
1 teaspoon salt
1/4 teaspoon pepper
3 pounds lamb shoulder, cut into 1-inch cubes
1 (15-ounce) can tomatoes with liquid
1 cup sour cream
1/4 cup finely chopped parsley

DUMPLINGS:
8 medium potatoes
2 eggs, lightly beaten
1 tablespoon salt
dash nutmeg
flour
croutons* for garnish

Prepare the stew: In a dutch oven, melt the butter or margarine and sauté the onions over medium heat until nearly tender. Meanwhile, mix together the paprika, salt, and pepper, then roll the lamb cubes in the seasonings. Brown the lamb with the onions; stir in tomatoes, cover, and simmer 2 hours, adding hot water if necessary to prevent burning. When lamb is tender, stir in sour cream and parsley; heat but do not boil.

Prepare the dumplings: Scrub but do not peel the potatoes; boil until tender. Cool, then peel and grate into a large bowl. Stir in eggs, salt, nutmeg, and enough flour to hold potatoes together. Drop heaping tablespoons of potato mixture into simmering salted water, without crowding, and cook 20 minutes. Remove dumplings with a slotted spoon to a serving bowl; garnish with croutons and serve with stew. Makes 6 to 8 servings.

* To make croutons: Blend minced garlic or herbs into butter or margarine, then spread onto slices of day-old bread. Cut the bread into cubes and bake at 300° F, stirring often, for 20 minutes or until brown.

ROAST STUFFED LEG OF LAMB

1/4 cup finely chopped parsley

3 scallions, trimmed and chopped

2 cloves garlic, finely chopped

1 tablespoon chopped fresh basil (or 1 teaspoon dried basil)

2 tablespoons olive oil

1 tablespoon lemon juice

1 teaspoon salt

1/4 teaspoon pepper

1 (6-pound) leg of lamb, bone removed

1 (1 to 1 1/2–pound) pork tenderloin

A variety of lamb dishes including
Roast Stuffed Leg of Lamb (bottom left)

Heat oven to 325° F. In a medium bowl, mix together parsley, scallions, garlic, basil, olive oil, lemon juice, salt, and pepper. Spread the lamb with the herb mixture, leaving 1/2-inch margins. Place the pork tenderloin on one long edge of the lamb, roll up jelly-roll style, and tie with kitchen string at 2-inch intervals. Place meat on a rack in a pan and roast uncovered about 2 1/2 to 3 hours, or until a meat thermometer registers 160° F. Makes 6 to 8 servings.

VEAL ROAST WITH VEGETABLE GRAVY

1 (4-pound) breast of veal
1 pound ground pork
1 cup soft breadcrumbs
2 onions, peeled and finely chopped
1 teaspoon salt
1/2 teaspoon pepper
2 eggs
1/2 cup finely chopped parsley
5 tablespoons unsalted butter
1 tablespoon oil
2 cloves garlic, finely chopped
1 1/2 cups dry white wine
1 carrot, peeled and finely chopped
1 stalk celery, finely chopped
1 tablespoon butter or margarine
mixed with 1 tablespoon flour, optional

Heat oven to 350° F. Cut a pocket in the veal for stuffing. In a large bowl, thoroughly blend ground pork, breadcrumbs, onions, salt, pepper, eggs, and parsley. Stuff mixture into the breast pocket and sew closed, using a darning needle and string or heavy thread. Melt butter or margarine with oil in a dutch oven; brown veal on all sides; add wine, cover, and place in oven for 1 hour. Remove cover and roast another 2 hours, basting every 15 minutes. One hour before roast is done, add chopped carrot and celery.

Remove roast to a heated platter; cover with foil to keep warm. Skim excess fat from juices in dutch oven, then boil over high heat until cooked down. If you like a thicker sauce, add the butter or margarine/flour mixture bit by bit, stirring until thickened. Makes 6 to 8 servings.

FISH FILLETS TO MAKE AND FREEZE

1 1/2 cups yellow cornmeal

1 cup grated Parmesan cheese

2/3 cup unsweetened toasted wheat germ

2 tablespoons garlic powder

2 tablespoons dried thyme, crushed

1 tablespoon dried sage

2 teaspoons salt

2 teaspoons pepper

4 eggs

1/3 cup milk

5 pounds very fresh fish fillets, such as cod, haddock, red snapper, catfish, pike, or trout

Fish Fillets

Have plenty of freezer wrapping paper handy. In a large plastic bag, shake together cornmeal, cheese, wheat germ, garlic powder, thyme, sage, salt, and pepper; set aside. In a large shallow bowl, beat together eggs and milk. Spread about half the cornmeal mixture out on a large platter. Dry fish fillets with paper towels; dip each into egg mixture and let drain briefly; dip into cornmeal mixture and turn to coat well on all sides. Replenish cornmeal mixture as needed.

Wrap fish with two layers of paper between each fillet to make them easy to separate. Label, seal in plastic bags, and freeze for up to 3 months. (Will make 10 servings.)

To cook 1 pound of breaded fillets: Do not thaw fish. Heat oven to 500° F. Melt 2 tablespoons butter or margarine and 2 tablespoons vegetable oil in a 9" x 13" pan. Turn frozen fillets in hot butter to coat, then bake, turning once, 12 to 18 minutes (time depends on thickness of fillets) or until fish flakes easily with a fork. Makes 4 servings.

HOT STEAK SANDWICHES

1 (5-pound) flank steak
olive oil
1 teaspoon salt or garlic salt
6 split sandwich rolls
Dijon mustard, optional

Heat oven to 375° F. Dry the steak with paper towels, then rub well with olive oil. Brush a large, heavy, ovenproof skillet with olive oil, then heat over high flame until smoking. Sprinkle steak with salt, then brown 2 minutes on each side. Place skillet in oven for 20 minutes. (Do not overcook or steak will be tough.) If you like, spread sandwich rolls with mustard. Remove steak to a board and carve against the grain into very thin slices; stack each roll with steak and serve hot. Makes 6 servings.

CORNED BEEF
AND CABBAGE

6 whole peppercorns
2 bay leaves
1 whole onion, peeled and stuck with 3 cloves
1 (5-pound) corned beef
1 head green cabbage, trimmed and cut into 8 wedges
8 carrots, peeled and cut into chunks
8 large red potatoes, unpeeled and cut into chunks
2 tablespoons butter or margarine

In a dutch oven, combine 2 quarts water, peppercorns, bay leaves, and onion. Wipe corned beef with paper towels; add to water. Boil over high heat for 10 minutes, then skim off scum and reduce heat to low. Cover and simmer about 4 hours or until tender; discard peppercorns, bay leaves, and onion.

About 40 minutes before beef finishes cooking, simmer cabbage, carrots, and potatoes in a large saucepan until tender. Drain and toss with butter or margarine.

Carve beef against the grain into thin slices and serve on a large platter with the vegetables. Makes 6 to 8 servings.

Corned Beef and Cabbage

ST. PATRICK'S DAY MENU

Beer-Cheese Spread*

Crackers and Cut Vegetables

Corned Beef and Cabbage*

Hot Rolls and Butter

Mixed Green Salad*

Apricot Pie*

Recipes can be found in this chapter.

CLASSIC AMERICAN MEATLOAF

1 1/2 pounds lean ground beef
1 cup regular or quick-cooking oatmeal, uncooked
2 teaspoons salt
1/4 teaspoon pepper
1 teaspoon prepared mustard
1 yellow onion, peeled and finely chopped
1/2 cup milk
1/4 cup ketchup

Heat oven to 350° F. In a large bowl, with your hands, mix all ingredients together with 1/4 cup water. Pack into a 9" x 5" loaf pan, mounding the top into a loaf shape. Bake uncovered 1 hour; let stand 10 minutes, drain off drippings, turn onto a platter, and slice. Makes 6 servings.

PEPPERED STEAKS

2 tablespoons black peppercorns
4 (1-inch-thick) filet mignon steaks
1/4 cup unsalted butter, softened
1 tablespoon finely chopped parsley
1 tablespoon lemon juice
1 teaspoon salt
4 tablespoons brandy

Crush peppercorns in a mortar and pestle or in a food processor, then press firmly into both sides of the steaks; let stand at room temperature for 30 minutes. Meanwhile, mix together butter, parsley, lemon juice, and salt; form into a log, wrap and refrigerate until needed.

Brush a large, heavy skillet lightly with oil, heat over high flame for 2 minutes, then reduce heat to medium-high. Add steaks and pan-broil, turning often (8 to 10 minutes for rare; 11 to 12 minutes for medium rare; 13 to 14 minutes for medium; and 15 to 16 minutes for well done).

Remove steaks to a warm platter. Cut butter log into four pieces and top each filet mignon with a butter pat. Pour brandy into skillet and heat, stirring up browned bits, for 1 minute, then pour over steaks. Makes 4 servings.

SIDE DISHES

OAT BRAN BREAKFAST MUFFINS

1 1/2 cups flour
1/2 cup regular or quick-cooking oatmeal, uncooked
1/2 cup oat bran
1 tablespoon baking powder
1/2 teaspoon salt
2 tablespoons sugar
1 1/4 cups milk
1 egg
3 tablespoons vegetable oil
additional oatmeal for topping, optional

Heat oven to 400° F. Grease the bottoms of 12 muffin cups or line with cupcake papers. In a large bowl, stir together flour, oatmeal, oat bran, baking powder, salt, and sugar. In a small bowl, beat together milk, egg, and oil. Pour egg mixture over the flour and stir quickly and lightly. Spoon batter into muffin cups, filling them 2/3 full. Sprinkle with additional oatmeal, if you like. Bake 20 minutes, or until a toothpick inserted in the center of a muffin comes out clean. Makes 12.

WILD THYME ASPARAGUS

1 pound fresh asparagus, trimmed
1/4 cup butter or margarine
1 clove garlic, crushed
1 tablespoon chopped parsley
1 teaspoon finely chopped onion
⅟ teaspoon finely chopped fresh thyme
1 teaspoon lemon juice
1/4 teaspoon salt

Steam asparagus until tender and keep warm. Meanwhile, melt butter or margarine and stir in garlic, parsley, onion, thyme, lemon juice, and salt; heat thoroughly. Place asparagus in serving bowl and pour on thyme sauce. Makes 4 servings.

CHEESE STICKS

2 cups flour
2 teaspoons salt
1/2 cup butter-flavored shortening
1 cup finely grated yellow cheddar cheese
milk
sesame or caraway seeds, optional

Heat oven to 425° F. Sift together flour and salt; cut in shortening with a pastry blender or two knives; stir in cheese. Gradually sprinkle in 4 to 6 tablespoons cold water, mixing gently until a ball forms. Roll out dough on a lightly floured surface to 1/8-inch thickness. Brush with milk and sprinkle with seeds, if desired. Cut into sticks or diamonds. Bake on cookie sheets 15 minutes or until golden brown. Makes about 3 dozen.

Oat Bran Breakfast Muffins

PINEAPPLE CITRUS PUNCH

1 (46-ounce) can pineapple juice

1 quart lemonade

1 quart orange juice

2 tablespoons unsweetened lime juice, fresh or frozen

1 lemon, thinly sliced

1 lime, thinly sliced

fresh pineapple spears for garnish, if desired

Chill all ingredients thoroughly before preparation. In a large punch bowl or pitcher, stir together pineapple juice, lemonade, orange juice, and lime juice. Add lemon and lime slices. Pour punch over tall glasses filled with ice cubes. Decorate with pineapple spears, if you like. Makes 10 servings.

Pineapple Citrus Punch

RED
POTATO
SALAD

1 cup sour cream

3 tablespoons cider vinegar or lemon juice

2 tablespoons sugar

1/2 teaspoon salt

1/2 teaspoon celery seed

6 medium red-skinned potatoes, boiled
and cut into cubes

4 eggs, hard-boiled, peeled
and cut into cubes

1 red onion, peeled and chopped

4 stalks celery, chopped

In a large bowl, stir together sour
cream, vinegar or lemon juice, sugar,
salt, and celery seed. Add potatoes,
eggs, onion, and celery; mix gently.
Chill before serving. Makes 6 servings.

MASHED
POTATO SALAD

2 cups cottage cheese

4 cups cold mashed potatoes

1/2 cup cooked and crumbled bacon

6 scallions, trimmed and chopped

1/4 cup chopped parsley

In a blender or food processor, puree
cottage cheese until smooth. In a large
bowl, mix together cottage cheese,
mashed potatoes, bacon, scallions, and
parsley. Taste to check seasonings and
add salt and pepper, if needed. Makes
8 servings.

Red Potato Salad

DESSERTS

BUNDT CAKE
WITH WHITE ICING

CAKE:
3 cups flour

1/2 cup unsweetened cocoa powder

1/2 teaspoon baking powder

1/2 teaspoon salt

1 cup milk

1 tablespoon vanilla

2 cups sugar

1 cup firmly packed brown sugar

1 cup butter or margarine, softened

1/2 cup shortening

5 eggs

ICING:
1 1/2 cups sugar

2 egg whites

1 tablespoon light corn syrup

1 teaspoon vanilla

Heat oven to 325° F. Grease and flour a bundt or tube cake pan. Sift together flour, cocoa powder, baking powder, and salt; set aside. In a small bowl, mix together milk and vanilla; set aside. In a large bowl, cream sugar, brown sugar, butter or margarine, and shortening until light and fluffy. Add eggs, one at a time, beating well after each addition. Add flour and milk mixtures alternately (beginning and ending with flour) to the sugar mixture; mix well. Pour into prepared pan and bake 1 hour 45 minutes or until the edges begin to pull away from the pan and a toothpick inserted in the center comes out clean. Cool 20 minutes in pan; invert onto cooling rack and cool completely.

When the cake is completely cool, begin making the icing. In the top of a double boiler, mix together sugar, egg whites, syrup, and 1/3 cup water. Set over simmering (not boiling) water and beat constantly with an electric mixer 4 to 7 minutes, or until white and fluffy. Remove from heat and add vanilla; continue beating until of good spreading consistency. Spread onto cake quickly. Makes 16 servings.

Bundt Cake with White Icing

OLD-FASHIONED CHOCOLATE PUDDING CAKE

1 cup flour
1 cup chopped walnuts
2/3 cup sugar
1/4 cup plus 2 tablespoons cocoa
1 teaspoon baking powder
1/4 teaspoon salt
2 tablespoons melted butter or margarine
1 teaspoon vanilla
1/2 cup milk
1 cup firmly packed brown sugar
1 3/4 cups boiling water

Heat oven to 350° F. Grease a shallow 1 1/2-quart baking dish or a 9" x 9" pan; set aside. In a bowl stir together flour, nuts, sugar, 2 tablespoons cocoa, baking powder, and salt. Mix melted butter, vanilla, and milk; lightly blend into flour mixture. Pour into pan; set aside. Mix brown sugar and remaining 1/4 cup cocoa and sprinkle over batter. Carefully pour boiling water over batter; do not mix. Bake 30 minutes. (A cake layer will be on top of a layer of pudding.) Serve immediately. Makes 4 to 6 servings.

THREE-LAYER LANE CAKE

CAKE:
1 cup butter, softened
2 cups sugar
3 1/4 cups flour
3/4 teaspoon salt
1 tablespoon baking powder
1 cup evaporated milk
1 teaspoon vanilla
8 egg whites

FILLING:
1 cup chopped pecans
2 cups sweetened coconut
1 cup chopped golden raisins
1/2 cup whiskey
8 egg yolks
1 cup sugar
1/2 cup butter, softened

Heat oven to 350° F. Grease three 9-inch round cake pans, line with wax paper, and lightly grease the wax paper; set aside. In a large bowl, cream butter and sugar until light and fluffy. In another bowl, stir together flour, salt, and baking powder. Add flour mixture to butter mixture alternately with milk and vanilla, beginning and ending with flour. Beat egg whites until stiff but not dry; fold into batter. Pour batter into pans and bake 25 to 30 minutes or until a toothpick inserted in the center comes out clean. Let cool 10 minutes before turning out onto racks to cool thoroughly. Pull off wax paper and discard.

To make the filling: Put nuts, coconut, raisins, and whiskey in a bowl; set aside. In the top of a double boiler, beat egg yolks until light. Gradually add sugar and butter; beat well. Place over simmering (not boiling) water and stir constantly until thickened. Fold nut mixture into thickened egg mixture. Spread filling over each of the three layers and stack them, or spread filling over two layers, then frost with White Icing (page 32). Makes 12 to 16 servings.

SPRING EGG CUSTARD

1 quart half-and-half or whole milk
2 tablespoons sugar
1 tablespoon vanilla
8 egg yolks
brown sugar for topping, optional

Heat oven to 300° F. Butter a 1 1/2-quart shallow baking dish or twelve custard cups; set aside. In a pan, scald half-and-half or milk, then stir in sugar and vanilla; set aside. In a large bowl, lightly beat egg yolks; slowly add hot milk to yolks, beating constantly. Pour mixture into baking dish or cups; place dish or cups in a larger pan and add warm water to a depth of 1 inch. Bake 1 hour or until a knife inserted halfway between the edge and the center comes out clean. Cool to room temperature, then chill thoroughly. Sprinkle with brown sugar, if desired, then place under broiler until sugar melts and caramelizes. Makes 12 servings.

Spring Egg Custard

LEMON JELLY CANDIES

Wrap these light little jewels individually in plastic wrap or cellophane for spring holiday gift giving.

2 packets unflavored gelatin
1 1/2 cups sugar
1 cup light corn syrup
1/2 teaspoon lemon juice
1/4 teaspoon lemon flavoring
few drops yellow food color
powdered sugar
cornstarch

Butter a 9" x 9" baking pan; set aside. Use a heavy pot with high sides for cooking because mixture will bubble up, and have a candy thermometer handy. In the pot, stir together gelatin and sugar, then slowly mix in 1 1/2 cups water and corn syrup. Over medium heat, stir constantly until sugar is dissolved, then cook uncovered, without stirring, to 222° F.

Set pot in a few inches of cold water in the sink and cool to 160° F. Stir in lemon juice, flavoring, and food color. Pour mixture into buttered pan and allow to cool to room temperature, then cover and refrigerate overnight.

Sprinkle a sheet of wax paper with powdered sugar and cornstarch, then gently turn jelly mixture out of pan onto the wax paper; sprinkle top with more sugar and cornstarch. Dip a knife in hot water and cut into 1-inch squares. Leave to dry 2 hours, then wrap individually. Makes 81 pieces.

LEMON MERINGUE PIE

4 egg yolks
1/2 cup cornstarch
1 1/4 cups sugar
1/4 teaspoon salt
1 tablespoon finely grated lemon zest
1/2 cup lemon juice
2 tablespoons butter or margarine
1 (9-inch) pie crust, baked and cooled

MERINGUE:
4 egg whites
1/4 teaspoon cream of tartar
1/8 teaspoon salt
1/2 cup sugar, sifted
1 teaspoon vanilla

Heat oven to 350° F. Lightly beat egg yolks in a small bowl; set aside. In a pan, stir together cornstarch, sugar, and salt. Gradually blend in 1 3/4 cups water until smooth. Cook over medium-high heat, stirring constantly, until mixture is thick and smooth. Remove from heat and stir in lemon zest. Stir a small amount of hot lemon mixture into egg yolks; return mixture to pan and cook, stirring, over low heat 2 or 3 minutes, but do not boil. Remove from heat and stir in lemon juice and butter or margarine. Pour filling into pie shell; set aside and make meringue.

In a grease-free bowl, beat together egg whites, cream of tartar, and salt until soft peaks form. With mixer running, gradually add sugar, and continue beating until stiff and shiny; stir in vanilla. Spread meringue over filling, forming peaks on top, and spreading meringue over the edges of the filling to seal. Bake 12 to 15 minutes, or until peaks are beginning to brown. Cool at least 2 hours before serving or serve chilled. Makes 6 servings.

APRICOT PIE

4 egg yolks
1/2 cup sugar
1 envelope unflavored gelatin
1/2 cup milk
2 teaspoons lemon juice
1 cup pureed apricots (or apricot baby food)
1 (9-inch) pie shell, baked and cooled, or graham cracker crumb crust
1/2 cup whipping cream, chilled

Beat egg yolks lightly in a small bowl; set aside. In the top of a double boiler, mix sugar, gelatin, and milk. Set over simmering (not boiling) water until steaming hot. Stir a small amount of hot milk mixture into egg yolks, then pour yolks into the pan and cook, stirring, 3 to 5 minutes or until thickened. Remove from heat and mix in lemon juice and apricot puree. Cool, stirring occasionally, until mixture mounds. In a cold bowl, whip cream until stiff, then fold into cooled apricot mixture. Spoon into pie shell and chill at least 4 hours before serving. Serve with additional whipped cream, if you like. Makes 6 to 8 servings.

Lemon Meringue Pie

BLUEBERRY CRUMB CAKE

CAKE:
1/4 cup butter or margarine

3/4 cup sugar

1 egg

2 cups flour

1/2 teaspoon salt

2 teaspoons baking powder

1/2 cup milk

2 cups fresh or frozen blueberries

CRUMB TOPPING:
1/2 cup firmly packed brown sugar

3 tablespoons flour

2 teaspoons cinnamon

3 tablespoons butter or margarine

1/2 cup chopped walnuts or pecans

Heat oven to 375°. Grease and flour a 10-inch springform pan; set aside. In a large bowl, cream together butter or margarine and sugar; beat in egg. Add flour, salt, baking powder, and milk; stir until well blended. Fold in blueberries carefully. Spoon into pan; set aside and make topping.

In a bowl, stir together brown sugar, flour, and cinnamon. With a pastry cutter or fork, blend in butter or margarine until crumbly; stir in nuts. Sprinkle topping over batter. Bake cake 40 to 50 minutes or until a toothpick inserted in the center comes out clean. Makes 8 to 10 servings.

**Blueberry
Crumb Cake**

CHAPTER TWO

SUMMER'S BOUNTY

*I*t's summertime and the living is outdoors, light, and warm. Long days, Little League, purple popsicles, hand-holding walks, steaks on the grill, family reunions, and relaxing fishing trips are just some of the things we look forward to.

Summer is often a very busy time on the farm, when growing crops and animals need extra attention. But even so, farm families take time during the long summer months to cook up some of their own or their neighbors' produce, get together to barbecue, or just sit on the porch in the evening, drink lemonade, and watch the sky change from light to dark.

This chapter offers a taste of the pleasures of summer, from party starters and snacks to entrees and side dishes designed for family, guests, and picnics, and desserts that are light and refreshing or hearty and filling.

All across the nation, folks in the country, suburbs, and cities kick off the summer with picnics and days at the beach or lake during Memorial Day weekend. Lots of swimming and fun makes people hungry, so take along a big basket of Southern Fried Chicken, Corn Salad, Red Potato Salad, cut raw vegetables, fresh rolls or biscuits and butter, and thick slices of Double Chocolate Loaf Cake.

Then, before you know it, mid-summer is marked by the Fourth of July. Some towns celebrate Independence Day with parades and picnics. In almost every corner of the country—from the Statue of Liberty to the Golden Gate Bridge—you can see fireworks as soon as it gets dark. Even if it's just sparklers in your own backyard, the Fourth is a time for being outside, for getting people together, and for grilling and barbecuing.

If your family doesn't have a traditional reunion to gather all the cousins for softball games, three-legged races, eating, and making videos and memories, consider planning one for a long weekend this summer. Put someone in charge of the menu, or ask each family group to contribute their own favorites for a big meal; you'll find plenty of suggestions for good-time food in this chapter.

SALADS, STARTERS, AND SOUPS

TOMATO SOUP WITH GARDEN BASIL

3 tablespoons vegetable oil
1 medium yellow onion, peeled and chopped
1 stalk celery, chopped
1 carrot, peeled and chopped
4 large, ripe tomatoes, peeled, seeded, and chopped
2 tablespoons chopped fresh basil
3 cups chicken or vegetable stock
2 tablespoons lemon juice
salt
chopped basil leaves for garnish, optional

In a large pan, heat oil and sauté onion, celery, and carrot until tender. Add tomatoes, basil, stock, and lemon juice. Simmer until tomatoes are soft. Taste for salt (the amount added depends on saltiness of stock). Serve as is, or cool slightly, then puree in blender or food processor. Reheat gently before serving. Garnish with chopped basil, if desired. Makes 8 to 10 servings.

COLD TOMATO SOUP

1 (1-pound, 12-ounce) can chopped tomatoes in puree
1 small green bell pepper, seeded and cut into chunks
1 small red bell pepper, seeded and cut into chunks
1 stalk celery, cut into chunks
3 scallions, roughly chopped
1/4 cup chopped parsley or cilantro
2 cloves garlic, peeled and minced
3 tablespoons olive oil
1 tablespoon balsamic or red wine vinegar
1 teaspoon sugar
1 teaspoon salt
1/4 teaspoon red pepper sauce (or to taste)

In a food processor or blender, puree tomatoes until smooth; pour into a large bowl. Process green pepper, red pepper, celery, scallions, parsley or cilantro, and garlic until chopped, but not smooth. Stir vegetables into tomatoes. Add olive oil, vinegar, sugar, salt, and pepper sauce; blend well. Cover bowl and refrigerate 24 hours before serving. Makes 4 to 6 servings.

STUFFED ARTICHOKES

6 medium artichokes (about 6 ounces each)
2 tablespoons lemon juice or white vinegar
1 tablespoon olive oil
1 small yellow onion, peeled and minced
1 or 2 cloves garlic, peeled and minced
2 medium red or white potatoes, boiled and diced small
1/4 cup chopped parsley or cilantro
3/4 teaspoon ground cumin
1/2 teaspoon salt
1/2 teaspoon pepper

Prepare artichokes by cutting off stems flush with bottoms, so they stand upright; with knife, make a shallow X in the bottom of each. Trim off tips of leaves with kitchen shears. Place artichokes upside down in a large steamer basket over water with lemon juice or vinegar added; steam until bottoms are tender and leaves pull out easily, about 30 minutes. Set aside to cool slightly, then gently spread leaves apart to reveal hairy choke at center. With your fingers and a spoon, pull the choke out and discard.

Meanwhile, heat oil in a large skillet and sauté onion and garlic until transparent. Stir in potatoes, parsley or cilantro, cumin, salt, and pepper; heat thoroughly. Stuff center and outer leaves of artichoke with potato filling. If you like, sprinkle with additional olive oil. Serve warm or at room temperature. Makes 6 servings.

MARINATED TOMATO-ONION SALAD

3 tablespoons olive oil
2 tablespoons cider vinegar
1 tablespoon sugar
1/2 teaspoon salt
6 medium ripe tomatoes, each cut into 8 wedges
1 medium red onion, cut in half and then into thin slices
1 large cucumber, peeled, seeded, and sliced
6 crisp inner leaves of romaine lettuce, shredded

In a medium bowl, stir together oil, vinegar, sugar, and salt. Add tomato, onion, and cucumber to oil mixture; toss. Cover and refrigerate 2 hours. Toss lettuce with salad or serve tomato mixture over lettuce on cold salad plates. Makes 6 to 8 servings.

Tomato Soup with Garden Basil

MELON AND SMOKED HAM

1 ripe melon, such as cantaloupe, honeydew, or crenshaw, chilled
12 paper-thin slices dry smoked ham,
such as Westphalian or prosciutto
freshly ground black pepper

Peel and seed melon; cut into 18 thin wedges. On cold salad plates, alternate slices of melon and ham; sprinkle lightly with pepper. Makes 6 servings.

VEGETABLE NOODLE SOUP TO MAKE AND FREEZE

4 pounds meaty beef bones
1/2 head green cabbage, finely shredded
4 stalks celery, chopped
2 onions, peeled and chopped
3 carrots, peeled and chopped
4 large tomatoes, peeled, seeded, and chopped
2 medium green peppers, seeded and chopped
1 (10-ounce) package frozen corn
1/4 cup minced parsley
1 (6-ounce) can tomato paste
1/4 cup ketchup or chili sauce
1 tablespoon salt
1 (8-ounce) package noodles

Heat oven to 400° F. In a large roasting pan, brown beef bones; remove from oven and place in large stock pot with 1 gallon of water. Cover and simmer 3 hours or until meat is falling from bones; remove and discard bones, leaving meat in the pot. Refrigerate broth until fat solidifies, then remove and discard fat. Cut up any large pieces of meat, add remaining ingredients except noodles, stir well, cover, and simmer 1 hour or until vegetables are tender. (Add hot water as necessary to maintain level.) Taste and adjust seasonings. Cool, then divide into freezer containers, label, and freeze for up to 6 months. To serve, prepare noodles according to package directions and add to hot soup. Makes about 8 quarts.

Vegetable Noodle Soup

Rare Flank Steak

MAIN DISHES

PEACHY HAM STEAK

1 (2 to 2 1/2-pound) ready-to-eat ham steak
1/4 cup butter or margarine
4 fresh peaches, peeled, pitted, and sliced into thin wedges
1 tablespoon sugar

In a large, heavy skillet, fry ham steak over medium heat about 3 minutes per side to brown lightly and heat through. Remove ham to a warm platter, cover with foil, and keep warm. Melt butter or margarine in same skillet; add peach wedges and sugar. Sauté, stirring often, about 8 minutes or until hot and glazed. Top ham with peaches and serve. Makes 4 servings.

Peachy Ham Steak

RARE FLANK STEAK

1 cup beer
1/4 cup olive oil
2 tablespoons red wine vinegar or cider vinegar
1 tablespoon prepared mustard
1 clove garlic, crushed
1 bay leaf, crumbled
1/2 teaspoon salt
1/4 teaspoon cayenne or black pepper
1 (3-pound) flank steak, scored on both sides with shallow cuts 1 inch apart

In a bowl, stir together beer, oil, vinegar, mustard, garlic, bay leaf, salt, and pepper. Place beef in a shallow, nonreactive dish and cover with marinade. Marinate at room temperature 4 hours, turning occasionally.

Grill over hot charcoal or broil in oven 3 inches from heat for 4 minutes per side. (Be sure marinated meat is at room temperature—not cold—at time of cooking. Do not overcook or meat will be tough.) Cut on diagonal, against the grain, in thin slices. Makes 6 servings.

SOUTHERN FRIED CHICKEN

1 frying chicken (3 to 3 1/2 pounds),
cut into pieces

1 cup milk or buttermilk

vegetable oil or shortening for frying

3/4 cup finely crushed soda crackers

1 tablespoon paprika

1/2 teaspoon baking powder

1/2 teaspoon garlic powder

1/4 teaspoon salt

1/4 teaspoon cayenne pepper
(or to taste)

1/2 cup flour

1 egg beaten with 1/4 cup milk

Cover chicken with 1 cup milk or buttermilk and let marinate for 1 hour.
Heat 1 inch oil or shortening in a large
heavy skillet to just below smoking
point. Meanwhile, place cracker
crumbs, paprika, baking powder, garlic powder, salt, and cayenne in a plastic or paper bag and shake well. Spread
flour on a plate and place egg/milk
mixture in a shallow bowl. Roll chick-
en pieces in flour, dip in egg/milk mixture, then place one or two chicken
pieces at a time in the bag and shake to
cover thoroughly.

Put dark chicken pieces first in hot
oil and fry 5 minutes before adding
white meat pieces, without crowding,
and continue frying for another 15 to
20 minutes, turning only once, until
well browned on all sides. Drain on
paper towels. Makes 4 to 6 servings.

Southern Fried Chicken

FRESH-CAUGHT TROUT WITH ALMONDS

1/2 cup flour
1 egg beaten with 1 tablespoon water
1/2 cup cornmeal or fine dry breadcrumbs
1/2 teaspoon salt
1/8 teaspoon pepper
1/4 cup vegetable oil
1/4 cup butter or margarine
3 pounds fresh trout fillets
1/2 cup slivered almonds
1 tablespoon lemon juice
2 tablespoons chopped parsley
lemon pieces, thinly sliced, for garnish

Spread flour on a plate, put egg and water in a shallow bowl, and mix cornmeal or breadcrumbs with salt and pepper in another shallow bowl. Heat oil and butter or margarine in a large skillet over medium heat. Pat fish dry with a paper towel, then coat each fillet with flour, dip into egg, and cover completely with seasoned cornmeal or breadcrumbs. Place fillets in hot oil/butter mixture and fry until brown on one side; turn and brown the other side (about 3 minutes on each side). Remove fish to a warm platter and cover with foil to keep warm.

Add almonds to hot oil and sauté until lightly brown, about 4 minutes. Remove almonds from oil with a slotted spoon and sprinkle onto fish. Sprinkle fish with lemon juice and parsley, garnish platter with lemon slices, and serve immediately. Makes 4 to 6 servings.

AVOCADO, SCALLION AND SOUR CREAM OMELET

4 strips bacon
2 tablespoons finely chopped yellow onion
3 scallions, chopped
2 tablespoons butter or margarine
5 eggs, lightly beaten
1/2 teaspoon salt
1/2 cup sour cream
1 ripe avocado, peeled and cut into thin wedges

In a large skillet, cook bacon until brown; drain and crumble; set aside. Discard all but 2 tablespoons of drippings. Sauté the onion and half the scallions until onion is transparent; remove. Wipe skillet, then melt butter or margarine in skillet. Stir salt into eggs, then pour into skillet. Cook over medium heat, lifting edges as omelet cooks to let uncooked egg flow underneath. When top of omelet looks moist and creamy, remove from heat and slide onto serving plate. Spoon sour cream on top, sprinkle with bacon and reserved scallion, and arrange avocado on top. Makes 3 or 4 servings.

SUMMER TURKEY SALAD

3/4 cup mayonnaise
2 tablespoons lemon juice
1 tablespoon prepared mustard
3 cups diced cold turkey
1/2 cup diced celery
1 ripe avocado, peeled and cubed
1 medium ripe tomato, coarsely chopped
paprika for garnish
lettuce leaves, optional

In a large bowl, mix together mayonnaise, lemon juice, and mustard. Stir in turkey, celery, avocado, and tomato. Sprinkle with paprika and serve on lettuce leaves, if you like. Makes 6 servings.

Summer Turkey Salad

Avocado, Scallion and Sour Cream Omelet

CHICKEN-ZUCCHINI BAKE

4 whole chicken breasts (1 pound each)
6 medium zucchini, cut into 1-inch chunks
1/3 cup butter or margarine
1/3 cup flour
2 3/4 cups chicken broth
4 cups shredded cheddar or Swiss cheese
2 tablespoons chopped scallions
1 cup fine dry breadcrumbs
2 tablespoons finely grated Parmesan cheese

Grease a shallow 9" x 13" baking pan; set aside. Place chicken breasts in a large skillet; cover with water and simmer 30 minutes. Meanwhile, steam zucchini until crisp-tender; drain well and set aside. Remove chicken from water, cool slightly, skin and bone chicken, and cut into chunks. Place chicken and zucchini in baking pan.

Heat oven to 350° F. In a medium pan, melt butter or margarine; blend in flour and stir until bubbly all over. Gradually add chicken broth and stir constantly until thickened. Remove from heat and add cheddar or Swiss cheese and scallions; stir until smooth. Pour over chicken and zucchini. Toss together breadcrumbs and Parmesan then sprinkle over sauce. Bake 25 to 30 minutes or until bubbly. Makes 6 to 8 servings.

MARYLAND FRIED CHICKEN

vegetable oil or shortening for frying
1 1/2 cups flour
1 1/2 teaspoons baking powder
1/2 teaspoon salt
1 egg
1 1/2 cups milk
3 tablespoons vegetable oil
2 small chickens (2 pounds each), cut into pieces

Heat 1 inch of vegetable oil or shortening in a large heavy skillet to just below smoking point. Meanwhile, in a medium bowl sift together flour, baking powder, and salt. In a small bowl, beat egg with milk and 3 tablespoons oil, then blend egg/milk mixture into flour mixture. Dip chicken pieces in batter, then fry 15 to 20 minutes, turning only once, until well browned on all sides. Drain on paper towels. (Note: Because batter-dipped chicken cooks slowly, use only small chickens.) Makes 4 to 6 servings.

Chicken-Zucchini Bake

COOKING
OUTDOORS

Cooking over a fire—
whether wood-, charcoal-, or
gas-fueled—is one of the
delights of summer. You can
give grilled meat, poultry, and
vegetables a terrific smoky
flavor by throwing packaged
wood chips onto the fire;
apple, mesquite, hickory,
and grape vine are some of
the woods on the market.
Or soak sawdust or shavings
in water for an hour, then
add them to the fire.

Never use pine, though,
which tastes of turpentine.

Marinades are another
way to add extra flavor to
grilled foods. Here's one to
use with beef, pork, lamb,
chicken, turkey, or vegetables—especially onions.

1 cup orange juice
1 cup ketchup
1/2 cup beer (preferably dark)
1/4 cup vegetable oil
1/4 cup honey
1 tablespoon soy sauce
1 teaspoon ginger
1 teaspoon concentrated smoke
flavoring, optional

Mix all ingredients. Marinate
food in a nonreactive pan up
to 6 hours, and use marinade
for basting during cooking.
Makes about 3 cups.

MIXED GRILL FOR A CROWD

1 (3-pound) chicken cut into pieces

4 shoulder pork chops, about 1/2 inch thick

1/2 cup lemon juice

1/2 cup vinegar

1/2 cup olive oil

3 cloves garlic, peeled and crushed

2 teaspoons mixed dried Italian herbs

1 pound sweet or hot Italian pork or turkey sausages

4 rib-eye steaks, about 3/4 inch thick

Arrange chicken pieces and pork chops in one layer in a shallow, nonreactive dish. In a bowl, stir together lemon juice, vinegar, olive oil, garlic, and herbs; pour over pork and chicken, cover, and refrigerate 4 hours; reserve marinade and use to baste chicken and pork during grilling. If sausages are not labeled "fully cooked," parboil covered in water for 15 minutes. Prepare outdoor grill by lighting charcoal. Cook meats over medium-hot coals, about 4 inches from heat, following chart:

Meat total cooking time

CHICKEN
30 to 45 minutes

PORK CHOPS
20 to 30 minutes

STEAKS
12 minutes for medium

SAUSAGES
10 minutes

Makes 10 to 12 servings.

Mixed Grill

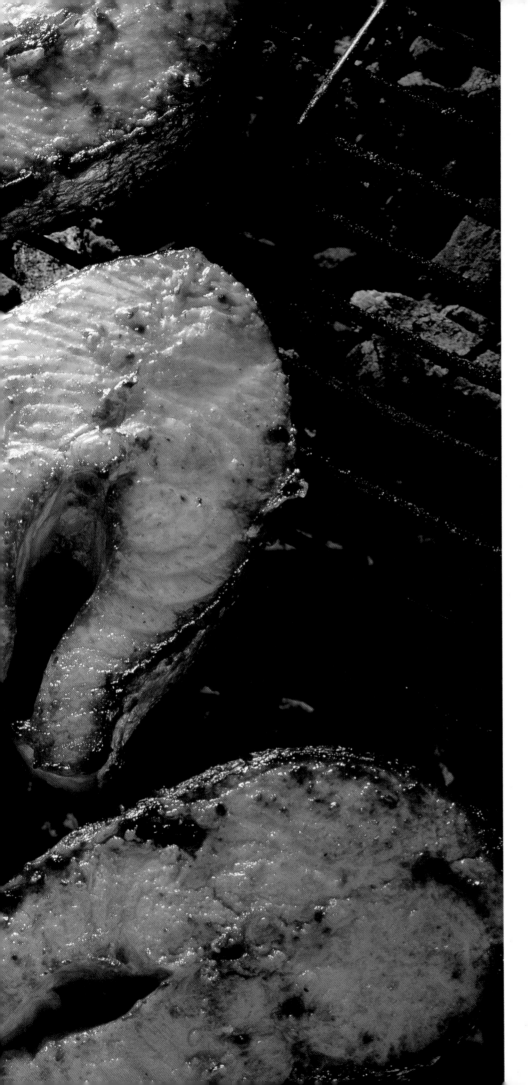

GRILLED SALMON STEAKS

4 salmon steaks (6 to 8 ounces each)

juice of 2 lemons (about 1/4 cup)

1/4 cup soy sauce

2 tablespoons sesame oil

1 tablespoon grated fresh ginger
or 1 teaspoon ground dried ginger

1 teaspoon finely grated lemon zest

At least 2 hours and up to 12 hours before serving, rinse salmon steaks in cold water and pat dry. Place fish in a large, flat, nonreactive dish; sprinkle with lemon juice, soy sauce, sesame oil, ginger, and lemon zest. Cover and refrigerate. Cook over moderately hot charcoal or gas grill, 5 to 8 minutes per side, until done. Makes 4 servings.

Grilled Salmon Steaks

Grilled Zucchini with Lemon and Rosemary

STIR FRY SAUCE

3 tablespoons soy sauce
2 teaspoons cornstarch
1 tablespoon cider vinegar
1 tablespoon honey

In a small bowl, gradually mix soy sauce into cornstarch; stir in remaining ingredients.

SUGAR SNAPS IN A SNAP

2 tablespoons butter or margarine
1 pound sugar snap peas, trimmed
1 English ("burpless") cucumber, thinly sliced
2 tablespoons chopped fresh mint
salt and pepper to taste

Melt butter or margarine in skillet or wok. Stir-fry sugar snaps and cucumber over high heat until crisp-tender. Toss in mint, salt, and pepper. Serve immediately. Makes 4 servings.

SIDE DISHES

GRILLED ZUCCHINI WITH LEMON AND ROSEMARY

1 tablespoon olive oil
1 tablespoon honey
2 teaspoons chopped fresh rosemary
8 small or 4 medium zucchini, cut in half lengthwise
1 lemon, thinly sliced
2 (6-inch) sprigs of fresh rosemary for garnish

In a small bowl, mix together oil, honey, and chopped rosemary. Brush mixture onto zucchini and lemon slices; cook on edges of medium-hot grill until lightly browned. Remove to serving platter and garnish with rosemary sprigs. Makes 4 servings.

ZUCCHINI WITH TOMATO SAUCE

2 tablespoons olive oil
6 medium zucchini, thinly sliced
1 cup chopped yellow onion
1 (15-ounce) can chopped tomatoes with Italian or Mexican seasonings, with juice
fresh herbs for garnish

Heat oil in large heavy skillet. Add zucchini and onion; sauté 3 to 5 minutes. Stir in tomatoes and their juice, cover, and simmer 5 minutes or until vegetables are tender. Garnish with fresh herbs, if you like. Makes 6 to 8 servings.

Zucchini with Tomato Sauce

SUMMER
VEGETABLE MEDLEY
TO MAKE AND FREEZE

5 pounds broccoli, trimmed and chopped

3 medium yellow onions, peeled and chopped

8 stalks celery, cut diagonally into 1-inch pieces

8 carrots, peeled and cut diagonally into 1-inch pieces

1 red bell pepper, cut into strips

1 green bell pepper, cut into strips

1 pound mushrooms, sliced

Fill a large stock pot with water and heat to boiling. Toss vegetables together in a large bowl; blanch in boiling water for 4 minutes; drain and plunge into cold water to stop cooking. Divide vegetables into four equal portions; place in freezer containers, label, and freeze for up to 3 months. (Will make 24 servings.)

To serve, stir-fry each portion in 2 tablespoons vegetable oil for 3 minutes, cover, and simmer another 3 minutes, then add Stir Fry Sauce (page 60), if you like; cook and stir until sauce is thickened and translucent. Makes 6 servings.

POTATO-CORN SALAD

3/4 cup white vinegar

1/3 cup sugar

1 teaspoon salt

3/4 teaspoon celery seeds

3 large red-skinned potatoes, peeled, boiled, and cut into cubes

1 cup corn kernels (cut from the cob and cooked, or canned and drained)

1/4 cup chopped green bell pepper

1/4 cup chopped red bell pepper

2 scallions, trimmed and chopped

In a pan, mix together vinegar, sugar, celery seeds, and mustard seeds; bring to a boil then reduce heat and simmer 5 minutes. Let cool. Gently stir in potatoes, corn, green pepper, red pepper, and scallions. Chill before serving. Makes 6 servings.

Potato-Corn Salad

POTATOES WITH CHEESE AND PARSLEY

4 medium potatoes, peeled and thinly sliced
1 small yellow onion, peeled and thinly sliced
1 cup grated cheddar cheese
3 tablespoons flour
1/4 cup chopped parsley
1 teaspoon salt
1/4 teaspoon pepper
2 cups milk, warmed

Heat oven to 350° F. Grease a 2-quart casserole or baking dish. Arrange potatoes and onion in four layers, sprinkling only the first three layers with cheese, flour, parsley, salt, and pepper. Carefully pour milk over the potatoes, cover tightly, and bake 30 minutes. Uncover and bake an additional hour. Makes 6 servings.

BUTTERMILK MASHED POTATOES

6 medium all-purpose potatoes
2 teaspoons salt (or to taste)
1/4 cup butter or margarine, softened
1/4 cup buttermilk or plain yogurt, at room temperature

Do not peel or puncture potatoes, but scrub well. Put potatoes and 1 teaspoon salt in large pan and cover with water. Bring to a slow boil and simmer 30 to 40 minutes or until potatoes are tender. Pour off water, peel potatoes, and return pan to heat to let potatoes dry a little. Add butter or margarine, buttermilk or yogurt, and remaining salt, then beat lightly with mixer or with potato masher until nearly smooth. Serve immediately. Makes 6 to 8 servings.

Buttermilk Mashed Potatoes

FLAVORED BUTTERS

Make summer meals and picnics even more fun by mixing up some quick flavored butters to serve on sweet breads, hot rolls, waffles, or muffins.

Cream 1/2 cup softened, unsalted butter or margarine until fluffy, then mix in one of the following:

- *1 tablespoon finely grated orange zest*

- *2 tablespoons strawberry jam*

- *2 tablespoons honey*

- *2 tablespoons maple syrup*

- *1 tablespoon finely minced fresh basil*

- *2 tablespoons brown sugar and 1/2 teaspoon cinnamon*

DESSERTS

DOUBLE CHOCOLATE LOAF CAKE

1 cup unsalted butter
1/2 cup shortening
3 cups sugar
5 eggs
3 cups flour
1/4 cup cocoa
1/2 teaspoon baking powder
1/2 teaspoon salt
1 cup milk
1 tablespoon vanilla
1 cup mini chocolate chips

Heat oven to 325° F. Grease and flour two 9" x 5" loaf pans; set aside. In a large bowl, cream together butter, shortening, and sugar until light and fluffy. Add eggs one at a time, beating well after each addition. Sift together flour, cocoa, baking powder, and salt. Stir together milk and vanilla. Add flour to butter mixture alternately with milk, beginning and ending with flour. Pour into pans and bake 1 hour or until a toothpick inserted in center comes out clean. Cool on racks 10 minutes, then turn out and cool completely. Makes 2 loaf cakes or about 20 servings.

LUSCIOUS CHERRY CHEESE CAKE

FILLING:
4 cups (2 pounds) whole-milk ricotta cheese
3/4 cup sugar
1/4 cup flour
4 eggs, beaten
1 tablespoon kirsch (cherry liqueur) or vanilla

CRUST:
1 cup flour
1/4 cup sugar
1 teaspoon baking powder
1/4 teaspoon salt
1/4 cup shortening

1 egg plus 1 egg white, beaten together
1/2 teaspoon vanilla

CHERRY SAUCE:
1 (15-ounce) can pitted sour red cherries
2/3 cup sugar
2 tablespoons cornstarch
few drops red food coloring, optional

The night before preparation, put two layers of cheesecloth or paper towels in a colander and let ricotta drain into a bowl in the refrigerator overnight; discard whey.

Prepare the crust: Lightly grease a 10-inch springform pan; set aside. In a bowl, stir together flour, sugar, baking powder, and salt. With two knives or a pastry blender, cut in shortening until it resembles coarse meal. Add egg and vanilla gradually, tossing with a fork until mixture holds together. Wrap in plastic and refrigerate 1 hour.

While pastry chills, prepare the filling: In a large bowl, mix together sugar, flour, drained ricotta cheese, eggs, and kirsch or vanilla until smooth. Cover and refrigerate until needed.

Heat oven to 375° F. Knead chilled pastry lightly seven or eight times, then roll out to an 11-inch circle. Fit into springform pan, patting edge of crust up sides of pan. Pour in cheese filling and bake 45 to 55 minutes or until filling is firm and the top is speckled with brown. Cool on a rack, then refrigerate at least 4 hours.

To make cherry sauce, drain cherries and reserve liquid. In a pan, mix sugar and cornstarch; blend in cherry liquid and food coloring, if desired. Heat, stirring, until thickened, then simmer 2 or 3 minutes. Add cherries; cool; refrigerate until needed. (If sauce is too thick after it cools, thin with a little water.) Serve chilled cake topped with cherry sauce. Makes 10 to 12 servings.

Double Chocolate Loaf Cake

Strawberry Shortcake

STRAWBERRY SHORTCAKE

SHORTCAKE:
2 cups flour

2 tablespoons sugar

1 tablespoon baking powder

1 teaspoon salt

1/2 cup shortening

3/4 cup milk

milk and sugar for glaze

TOPPING:
2 quarts strawberries, sliced

3/4 cup superfine sugar

1 cup heavy cream, whipped

Heat oven to 425° F. Grease a baking sheet; set aside. In a large bowl, stir together flour, sugar, baking powder, and salt. With two knives or a pastry blender, cut shortening into flour mixture until it resembles coarse meal. Quickly mix in milk with a fork, until just blended. Knead gently on a lightly floured board and roll to 1/2 inch thick. Cut with a large (3-inch) biscuit cutter and place on baking sheet, barely touching. Brush cakes with milk, then sprinkle with sugar. Bake 15 minutes or until light brown. Let cool. (Makes 10 to 12 shortcakes.)

To make topping, lightly crush strawberries with a fork or potato masher; stir in sugar; set aside until sugar melts.

To serve: split shortcakes with a fork; spoon strawberries and juice onto bottoms of shortcakes; cover with shortcake tops and spoon on whipped cream. Makes 10 to 12 servings.

PURPLE PLUM TART

SHELL:

1 1/2 cups flour

1/4 cup sugar

1/2 teaspoon salt

3/4 cup shortening

1 egg yolk

1/2 teaspoon white vinegar

3 tablespoons milk

FILLING:

1/2 pound cream cheese, softened

3 tablespoons sugar

2 tablespoons orange or apple juice

1 teaspoon vanilla

FRUIT TOPPING:

1/2 cup red currant jelly

2 tablespoons orange or apple juice

1 tablespoon butter or margarine

12 to 15 ripe purple plums, pitted and cut into thin wedges

First, prepare the shell: Lightly grease a 10-inch tart pan with removable bottom; set aside. In a bowl, stir together flour, sugar, and salt; with two knives or a pastry blender, cut shortening into flour mixture until it resembles coarse meal. In a

Purple Plum Tart

small bowl, stir together egg yolk, vinegar, and milk. Quickly and lightly stir milk mixture into flour mixture just until it holds together. Cover and refrigerate for 1 hour.

Heat oven to 375° F. Gently knead dough seven or eight times, then roll out on a lightly floured board. Transfer to tart pan, press into edges of pan, and trim. Prick the bottom of the pastry with a fork several times. Bake 15 minutes or until lightly browned. Set aside to cool completely.

While shell is cooling, make the filling. Beat together cream cheese, sugar, orange or apple juice, and vanilla using an electric mixer. Spread into cooled crust and chill 30 minutes.

To make the fruit topping, in a small saucepan melt jelly with orange or apple juice and butter or margarine; set aside to cool. Arrange plum wedges on top of cream cheese filling in overlapping concentric circles. Gently brush with cooled glaze; refrigerate 2 hours before serving. Makes 12 servings.

HONEY RAISIN BREAD

2 3/4 cups flour

2 1/2 teaspoons baking powder

1/2 teaspoon baking soda

1/2 teaspoon salt

2 tablespoons butter or margarine, softened

1 cup honey

1 egg

3/4 cup orange juice

3/4 cup raisins

1/2 cup chopped walnuts or pecans, optional

Heat oven to 325° F. Grease and flour a 9" x 5" loaf pan; set aside. Sift together flour, baking powder, baking soda, and salt; set aside. In a bowl, cream butter or margarine and honey; beat in egg. Add flour alternately with orange juice, beginning and ending with flour. Stir in raisins and nuts. Spoon into loaf pan and bake 1 1/4 hours or until a toothpick inserted near the center comes out clean. Let cool in pan 10 minutes, then turn out onto wire rack to cool completely. Wrap well and keep overnight before slicing. Makes 8 to 10 servings.

Honey Raisin Bread

AUNT FANCY'S BERRY TART

2/3 cup sugar

1/3 cup flour

1/8 teaspoon salt

2 cups milk

2 eggs

1 teaspoon vanilla

1 (15-ounce) package brownie mix, prepared according to package directions, but baked in a 10-inch round cake or springform pan

3 cups assorted fresh berries, whole and sliced

1/2 cup red currant jelly or apricot jam

In a pan, mix sugar, flour, and, salt. Gradually stir in milk and heat, stirring constantly, until thickened and bubbly. Beat eggs in a bowl; stir in a small amount of hot milk mixture then return to pan and heat 1 minute longer (do not boil). Stir in vanilla. Cool, stirring often. Pour onto prepared brownie base and arrange berries on top. Melt jelly or jam in a pan or in microwave. (Strain apricot jam.) Brush melted jelly or jam over fruit. Chill 2 hours before serving. Makes 6 servings.

PICNIC FRUIT SALAD

1 pint strawberries, sliced

1 pint blueberries

3 kiwi fruit, peeled and sliced

1 medium cantaloupe, peeled, seeded, and cut into balls or chunks

1 medium honeydew melon, peeled, seeded, and cut into balls or chunks

1/2 cup orange juice

1/4 cup lemon juice

2 tablespoons powdered sugar

mint leaves for garnish

In a large bowl, toss together strawberries, blueberries, kiwi fruit, cantaloupe, and honeydew; cover and refrigerate until chilled. In a small jar, shake together orange juice, lemon juice, and sugar. Pour orange juice mixture over fruit and garnish with mint leaves just before serving. Makes 8 to 10 servings.

Aunt Fancy's Berry Tart

Watermelon Ice Crush

WATERMELON ICE CRUSH

1 cup sugar

2 tablespoons lemon juice

2 cups crushed watermelon, seeded

In a pan, bring 3 cups water and sugar to a boil; reduce heat and simmer 5 minutes; let cool. Stir in lemon juice and watermelon; pour into a 9" x 13" pan, cover and place in freezer. Freeze to a mush; stir well; freeze until firm and stir again before serving. Makes 8 to 10 servings.

CHAPTER THREE

AUTUMN'S HARVEST

As nice as summer is, by the time September and October roll around we're usually ready for a little nip in the air and cooler days and nights. The full bounty of summer is realized in the autumn when harvests are brought in. It's a time of pumpkins and other winter squash, broccoli, sweet potatoes, apples, pears, and fresh baked goods made from newly ground whole wheat.

Appetites sometimes change with the seasons and we want to indulge in the fruits, vegetables, and meats of autumn after the lightness of summer meals. But that doesn't necessarily mean we want to spend more time in the kitchen every day. If you'd like to prepare a quick meal that's a little different from the norm around your house, try Mushroom Barley Soup served with corn muffins, or Stove-Top Sausage Stew with a carrot and raisin salad that you can pick up from a salad bar on your way home from work.

Is Labor Day the end of summer, the beginning of autumn, or a little of both? However you look at it, Labor Day weekend for many people is the last chance of the year to take the boat out, set up a tent in the mountains, or light the barbecue grill. It often marks the beginning of the school year, which for many adults as well as children is a time for making new plans and resolutions.

Especially for families with children, Halloween is a special day and is the second-biggest party night of the year—topped only by New Year's Eve. Get in on the fun and plan a costume party this Halloween, with lots of Scrumptious Carrot Cake and Spicy Grape Punch on hand.

By the end of the season, Jack Frost will be seen in many parts of the country. Thanksgiving is a favorite holiday, because it's a time to count our blessings and gather strength for the Christmas holiday and the turn of the year. We have only this one day each year when the whole nation sets aside time to give thanks and appreciate another wonderful harvest from the earth. Enjoy it.

❖ ❖ ❖ ❖ ❖ ❖ ❖ ❖ ❖ ❖ ❖ ❖ ❖ ❖ ❖

Three-Bean Salad

SALADS, STARTERS, AND SOUPS

THREE-BEAN SALAD

1/2 cup olive oil
1/3 cup vinegar
3 tablespoons sugar
1 teaspoon salt
1/8 teaspoon pepper
1 (15-ounce) can cut wax beans, drained
1 (15-ounce) can cut green beans, drained
1 (15-ounce) can red kidney beans, drained
1 cup minced yellow onion
1 cup minced green pepper

In a bowl, whisk together oil, vinegar, sugar, salt, and pepper. Add wax beans, green beans, kidney beans, onion, and green peppers; toss together. Cover and refrigerate several hours or overnight. Makes 6 to 8 servings.

MARINATED MUSHROOM AVOCADO SALAD

1 clove garlic, peeled
1/2 teaspoon salt
1 teaspoon prepared mustard
2 tablespoons lemon juice
1/2 cup olive oil
2 tablespoons chopped parsley or cilantro
3/4 pound mushrooms, sliced
1 large ripe avocado, peeled and cut in cubes
6 or 8 lettuce leaves
parsley or cilantro sprigs for garnish

In a small bowl, mash garlic and salt together; beat in mustard, lemon juice, oil, and parsley or cilantro until well blended. Place mushrooms and avocado in a medium bowl; pour marinade over, cover, and refrigerate 1 hour. Serve on lettuce leaves garnished with sprigs of parsley or cilantro. Makes 6 to 8 servings.

**Mushroom
Barley Soup**

MUSHROOM BARLEY
SOUP

1/4 cup butter or margarine
1 large yellow onion, peeled and chopped
1 cup pearl barley
1 carrot, peeled and chopped
2 cups chopped or sliced mushrooms
6 cups beef or chicken broth
2 bay leaves
salt and pepper to taste

In a pan, melt butter or margarine and sauté
onion about 5 minutes or until transparent; add
barley and continue cooking another 2 minutes.
Add carrot, mushrooms, broth, and bay leaves;
cover loosely and simmer 1 to 1 1/2 hours or
until barley is tender. Taste and adjust seasoning. Remove bay leaves before serving. Makes 6
to 8 servings.

NEW ENGLAND
CLAM CHOWDER

1/4 cup butter or margarine
1 large yellow onion, peeled and minced
2 cans clams (10 ounces each)
2 medium potatoes, peeled and diced
1 teaspoon salt
3 cups milk
paprika or chopped parsley for garnish

Melt butter or margarine in a pan and sauté onions about 5
minutes or until transparent; add liquid from clams, potatoes, and salt; cover and simmer 10 minutes or until potatoes are tender. Add clams and milk; cook 5 minutes or until
heated through, but do not boil. Garnish each serving with
paprika or parsley, if you like. Makes 6 to 8 servings.

New England Clam Chowder

CHEDDAR CHEESE SOUP

2 large potatoes, peeled and diced
2 large carrots, peeled and diced
1 large yellow onion, peeled and diced
2 tablespoons butter or margarine
3 cups milk
1 cup grated sharp cheddar cheese
1 teaspoon salt
chopped parsley and/or freshly ground
black pepper for garnish

In a pan, cover potatoes and carrots with water and cook about 8 minutes or until tender; let cool slightly. Meanwhile, in a small skillet, sauté onion in butter or margarine. In a blender or food processor, puree potatoes, carrots, and onion with the cooking liquid. Return puree to pan; add milk, cheese, and salt; heat thoroughly, but do not boil, until cheese is melted. Garnish each serving with parsley and/or pepper. Makes 6 to 8 servings.

BITE-SIZED PARTY BISCUITS

2/3 cup flour
1/3 cup grated sharp cheddar cheese
2 tablespoons butter or margarine
2 to 3 tablespoons milk or buttermilk
melted butter or margarine for glaze

Heat oven to 400° F. Grease an 8" x 8" baking pan. In a bowl, mix flour and cheese; with two knives or a pastry blender, cut in butter or margarine until mixture resembles coarse meal. Stir in enough milk to form a stiff dough. Roll out on a floured board to 1/2 inch thick. Cut with a small (1-inch) biscuit cutter; place rounds on cookie sheet; brush tops with melted butter or margarine. Bake 8 to 10 minutes or until golden brown. Serve warm, or cool, wrap, and freeze. (Re-heat cooled or frozen biscuits wrapped in foil.) Makes about 3 dozen.

Cheddar Cheese Soup

FLAVORFUL VEGETABLE STEW TO MAKE AND FREEZE

Make the most of your end-of-the-season garden vegetables by fixing a big batch of this versatile blend, then freezing it to use throughout the winter on pasta, pork chops, quiche, or as a side dish.

2 eggplants, peeled and cubed
6 zucchini, coarsely chopped
1 tablespoon salt
1/2 cup olive oil
4 yellow onions, peeled and chopped
2 green bell peppers, chopped
2 red bell peppers, chopped
10 ripe tomatoes, peeled, seeded, and chopped
1/2 cup minced parsley
1 teaspoon sugar

Sprinkle eggplants and zucchini with 2 teaspoons salt and place in a colander to drain for 1 hour. Heat oil in a large, heavy pot and sauté onions and peppers until onion is golden. Add eggplant, zucchini, remaining salt, tomatoes, parsley, and sugar. Simmer, covered, for 30 minutes, then uncover and continue cooking another 40 minutes or until most of liquid is cooked away and mixture is thick. Taste and correct seasoning. Cool to room temperature, then pack in freezer containers, label, and freeze. Makes about 3 quarts.

AUTUMN

Autumn can be a busy time as harvests come in, children go back to school, and holiday preparations begin. Warm, nutritious meals that are quick to prepare and require minimum clean-up are the way to go. Here are some menus that fit the bill.

Macaroni and Cheese with Bacon*

Steamed Broccoli

Baked Apples with Honey and Raisins*

Spicy Catfish*

Stewed Tomatoes

Baked Rice Supreme*

Scrumptious Carrot Cake* Topped with Warm Applesauce

Pan-Fried Ham Steak

Stuffed Acorn Squash*

Steamed Green Beans Indian Pudding* with Ice Cream

Recipes marked with an asterisk (*) can be found in this chapter.

MAIN DISHES

MACARONI AND CHEESE WITH BACON AND BROCCOLI

1/2 pound macaroni, cooked according to
package directions and drained
6 strips bacon, cooked crisp and crumbled
1 (10-ounce) package frozen broccoli florets,
cooked according to package directions, and drained
1 1/2 cups cottage cheese
1 cup sour cream
1 small yellow onion, peeled and minced
1 tablespoon ketchup

Heat oven to 350° F. Grease a 1 1/2-quart baking dish; set aside. In a bowl, mix all ingredients together; spoon into baking dish. Bake 45 minutes or until golden brown and bubbly. Makes 8 servings.

CREAMY SPINACH-EGG SUPPER

2 packages frozen chopped spinach (10 ounces each)
1/4 cup butter or margarine
1/4 cup flour
2 cups milk
1/2 teaspoon salt
1/8 teaspoon pepper
1/4 teaspoon nutmeg
1/2 cup finely grated Parmesan cheese
6 eggs
additional Parmesan for topping

Heat oven to 350° F. Grease a 1-quart baking dish; set aside. Cook spinach according to package directions; drain well and set aside.

Meanwhile, make sauce: in a pan, melt butter or margarine and stir in flour; cook, stirring, until bubbly. Gradually stir in milk; add salt, pepper, and nutmeg; stir until smooth and beginning to thicken. Stir in 1/2 cup Parmesan, a few tablespoons at a time, until smooth; let simmer 2 or 3 minutes.

Spread spinach evenly in baking dish, and with a spoon form 6 depressions in the spinach. Slip an egg in each depression. Carefully pour hot sauce over eggs; sprinkle with additional cheese. Bake uncovered 15 minutes. Broil a few minutes until top is speckled with brown. Makes 6 servings.

Macaroni and Cheese with Bacon and Broccoli

SPICY CATFISH

3 pounds catfish fillets
1/2 teaspoon salt
1/2 teaspoon paprika
1/4 teaspoon black pepper
1/4 teaspoon cayenne pepper
2 cloves garlic, peeled and minced
3 tablespoons lemon juice or vinegar

Heat oven to 400° F. Tear off a large piece of heavy-duty aluminum foil; lightly oil foil and lay fish on it; set aside. In a small bowl, mix salt, paprika, pepper, and cayenne; mash in garlic with a fork and stir in lemon juice or vinegar. Pour sauce over fish and wrap foil tightly. Place foil package in a baking dish and bake 30 minutes or until fish flakes easily with a fork. Makes 6 servings.

HEARTY HAM AND POTATO STEW

4 large all-purpose potatoes, peeled and diced
2 tablespoons butter or margarine
3 tablespoons flour
6 scallions, chopped, including green tops
2 cups milk
3 cups cooked ham, cubed
1 (15-ounce) can cream-style corn

In a large pot, boil potatoes only until done, about 10 minutes; remove and drain; set aside. In the same pot, melt butter or margarine and stir in flour; cook until bubbly; add scallions and cook another 2 minutes. Stir in milk and 2 cups water; cook, stirring constantly, until boiling and slightly thickened. Add potatoes, ham, and corn; heat thoroughly. Makes 6 to 8 servings.

Spicy Catfish

CHICKEN AND VEGETABLES IN A POT

1 whole chicken (3 to 3 1/2 pounds)
2 tablespoons vegetable oil
1/2 lemon
4 bay leaves
6 baby artichokes, halved
12 small whole onions, peeled
6 whole garlic cloves, unpeeled
6 small red potatoes, halved
4 carrots, peeled and cut into pieces
1/2 cup dry white wine or chicken stock
1 teaspoon salt
1/4 teaspoon freshly ground black pepper

Heat oven to 375°F. Rinse and dry chicken, and place lemon half and two bay leaves inside cavity. Tie legs together. Rub oil over entire chicken and place in a clay pot, deep casserole, or roasting pan. Add remaining ingredients to pot, including extra bay leaves. Bake, covered, for 1 1/2 hours. (Check after 1 hour: if chicken is not browning, remove cover for the last 30 minutes of cooking time.) Remove lemon before serving. Pour liquid from pot into a bowl and skim fat from surface. Taste gravy for seasoning and correct. Serve chicken surrounded by vegetables. Makes 6 to 8 servings.

Chicken and Vegetables in a Pot

HOLIDAY STUFFED TURKEY

1 cup butter
1 medium yellow onion, peeled and chopped
4 stalks celery with leaves, chopped
2 teaspoons salt
1 teaspoon dried sage
1 teaspoon dried thyme, crushed
1/2 teaspoon pepper
9 cups soft bread cubes
1 cup chopped dried apricots
1 cup chopped pecans
1 12-pound oven-ready turkey
oil for basting

Heat oven to 325° F. Melt butter in a large skillet or pan; sauté onion and celery until soft. Stir in salt, sage, thyme, and pepper. Add bread cubes, apricots, and pecans; mix well. Remove giblets and neck from turkey. Stuff turkey immediately before roasting, not earlier. Truss turkey and fold wings under body. Place stuffed turkey breast side up on a roasting rack in a baking pan; baste with oil. Roast 4 1/2 to 5 hours, basting occasionally. (To prevent skin from burning, loosely cover with foil when skin begins to brown.) Turkey is done when meat thermometer registers 185° F or when drumstick moves very easily. Allow turkey to stand 20 minutes before slicing. Immediately after serving, remove any remaining stuffing from cavity, wrap, and refrigerate separately. Makes 12 servings.

Holiday Stuffed Turkey

BBQ RIB DINNER

1 cup soy sauce

1 cup brown sugar

1 tablespoon grated fresh ginger
or 1 teaspoon ground dried ginger

4 cloves garlic, crushed

4 to 5 pounds lean pork spareribs, cut in 2-rib portions

In a large, shallow, nonreactive baking dish, mix soy sauce, sugar, 1 cup water, ginger, and garlic until sugar dissolves. Add ribs and turn to distribute marinade. Cover dish and refrigerate at least 4 hours and up to 12 hours, turning occasionally.

Heat oven to 350° F. Bake ribs, uncovered, in marinade for 2 hours, turning every half hour, until tender. Makes 4 servings.

STOVE-TOP SAUSAGE STEW

1 pound sweet or hot Italian pork or turkey sausages

1 large yellow onion, peeled and chopped

2 carrots, peeled and chopped

1/2 cup chopped parsley

1 teaspoon dried sage

1 (15-ounce) can white kidney beans, drained and rinsed

3 cups beef broth or water

salt and pepper to taste

Remove casings from sausages and crumble into a pan; cook until browned; drain all but 2 tablespoons fat. Add onion and carrots; sauté until onion begins to turn golden. Stir in parsley, sage, beans, broth or water, salt, and pepper. Simmer about 10 minutes. Makes 4 to 6 servings.

CHICKEN BREASTS ON NOODLES

6 chicken breast halves, skin and bones removed

salt and pepper

1/4 cup butter or margarine

12 ounces noodles

2 cups meatless spaghetti sauce

3 teaspoons finely minced garlic

1 teaspoon dried oregano, crushed

1/2 cup grated Parmesan cheese

Sprinkle chicken with salt and pepper. Melt butter or margarine in large skillet and brown chicken on all sides until cooked through; remove from skillet, set aside, and keep warm. Meanwhile, cook noodles according to package directions; drain well. Heat spaghetti sauce in a small pan; set aside. Over low heat, sauté garlic in butter remaining in skillet. Do not brown garlic. Add oregano and stir in cooked noodles and 1 cup spaghetti sauce; heat thoroughly. Arrange noodles on a serving platter; top with chicken breasts and remaining hot spaghetti sauce; sprinkle with Parmesan cheese. Makes 6 servings.

BBQ Rib Dinner

Chicken Breasts on Noodles

BONELESS PORK CHOPS WITH RED POTATOES

1/4 cup vegetable oil or bacon drippings

1 1/2 pounds small red potatoes, scrubbed and cut into wedges

6 boneless shoulder pork chops, about 1/2 inch thick

salt and pepper

Dijon mustard

2 tablespoons vegetable oil

1/2 cup dry white wine

Heat oven to 400° F. Place oil or drippings in an 11" x 7" baking dish and heat in oven until hot. Place potatoes in hot oil, turn to coat, and place in oven; bake 30 minutes or until potatoes are golden and crunchy.

Meanwhile, season chops with salt and pepper and spread with a light coating of mustard. Heat 2 tablespoons oil in a large skillet; add chops and sauté until done, about 7 minutes on each side; transfer to a serving platter and keep warm.

Pour wine into skillet and deglaze by scraping up browned bits; cook over high heat to reduce to about 1/3 cup. Pour sauce over chops and surround chops with potatoes. Serve with additional mustard, if you like. Makes 6 servings.

Boneless Pork Chops with Red Potatoes

SIDE DISHES

GREEN BEANS WITH WALNUTS AND BLUE CHEESE

1 pound green beans, trimmed and cut into 2-inch lengths

2 tablespoons olive oil

1 clove garlic, peeled and minced

1 tablespoon chopped parsley

1/2 cup chopped toasted walnuts

1/2 cup crumbled blue cheese

Parboil green beans by dropping into boiling water and simmering for 10 minutes or just until barely tender; drain well. Heat oil in a large skillet over high heat; add green beans and stir-fry 4 minutes or until just beginning to color; stir in garlic and stir-fry 1 minute. Remove from heat and stir in parsley, walnuts, and blue cheese. Serve immediately. Makes 4 servings.

MUFFINS TO MAKE AND FREEZE

3 cups whole wheat flour

2 1/4 cups all-purpose flour

1/2 cup sugar

3 tablespoons baking powder

2 teaspoons salt

3 eggs, lightly beaten

3 cups milk

1/2 cup vegetable oil

Variations (optional):

3 tablespoons finely grated orange zest; 2 cups raisins, chopped dates, or dried currants; 2 cups chopped walnuts or pecans; or 3 cups fresh or frozen blueberries

Heat oven to 425° F. Place cupcake papers in 36 muffin cups. In a very large bowl, stir together whole wheat flour, all-purpose flour, sugar, and salt. Add choice of one variation ingredient, if desired. In another bowl, stir together eggs, milk, and oil. Make a well in dry ingredients and pour milk mixture in center; stir quickly and lightly just to moisten. Batter should be lumpy. Spoon batter into cupcake papers, 2/3 full. Bake 20 minutes or until golden and peaked. Remove from pans and cool completely on racks. Wrap well for freezing and label. Freeze for up to 3 months. To thaw, leave at room temperature, still wrapped, 2 hours. Makes 36 muffins.

Green Beans with Walnuts and Blue Cheese

Assorted Muffins

STUFFED ACORN SQUASH

2 acorn squash (1 pound each), cut in half
lengthwise and seeded
1/2 cup rich cracker crumbs
1/2 cup chopped walnuts or pecans
2 tablespoons brown sugar
2 tablespoons melted butter or margarine

Heat oven to 375° F. Place squash halves in baking dish; cover with foil and bake 30 minutes. Meanwhile in a bowl, mix together cracker crumbs, nuts, sugar, and butter or margarine. Uncover squash and sprinkle filling equally into depressions in squash. Bake uncovered another 20 minutes. Makes 4 servings.

BAKED RICE SUPREME

1/4 cup butter
1 medium onion, peeled and chopped
1/2 cup chopped celery
2 tablespoons chopped scallions
1 1/2 cups uncooked long-grain white rice
1/2 teaspoon salt
3 cups chicken broth or water
2 tablespoons chopped parsley

Heat oven to 350° F. In an ovenproof 1 1/2- or 2-quart pan or casserole, melt butter. Sauté onion, celery, scallions, and rice until onions are tender and rice is golden. Stir in salt and chicken broth or water; cover tightly. (If lid does not fit tightly, cover pan with foil first.) Bake 25 to 30 minutes or until liquid is absorbed. Fluff with a fork and add parsley. Makes 8 servings.

ROASTED SWEET AND WHITE POTATOES

1/2 cup melted bacon drippings or vegetable oil
3 medium all-purpose or Idaho potatoes, each peeled and cut into 8 wedges
3 medium sweet potatoes, each peeled and cut into 8 wedges
1 teaspoon salt

Heat oven to 400° F. Put drippings or oil in a roasting pan or shallow baking dish. Turn potatoes in fat to coat all sides. Bake 45 minutes or until golden and tender. Drain on paper towels and sprinkle with salt; serve immediately. Makes 6 to 8 servings.

CRANBERRY RELISH

2 cups cranberries
2 seedless oranges, cut into eighths
2 small Granny Smith apples, peeled, cored, and cut into eighths
1 cup sugar

Put all ingredients in a food processor and chop coarsely, or grind fruit through the coarsest blade of a food grinder, then add sugar. Place ingredients in a glass or ceramic bowl, cover, and refrigerate 6 hours before serving. Makes about 1 quart.

SPICY GRAPE PUNCH

2 quarts apple juice
2 quarts purple or white grape juice
2 teaspoons whole cloves
2 teaspoons whole allspice
2 cinnamon sticks

In a large pan, heat all ingredients, cover and simmer 20 minutes. Strain before serving. Makes 1 gallon.

DESSERTS

INDIAN PUDDING

3 cups milk, heated to scalding
2/3 cup molasses
1/4 cup butter or margarine
1/3 cup yellow cornmeal
1/3 cup sugar
1 teaspoon salt
1 teaspoon ginger
1/2 teaspoon cinnamon
1/2 teaspoon nutmeg
1 cup cold milk
2 eggs, lightly beaten

Heat oven to 300° F. Grease a 2-quart casserole or baking dish. Stir molasses and butter or margarine into hot milk in pan. Over low heat, gradually add cornmeal, sugar, salt, ginger, cinnamon, and nutmeg, stirring constantly until thickened—about 10 minutes. Stir together cold milk and eggs; stir into cornmeal mixture. Spoon into casserole. Bake 2 hours or until a knife inserted midway between edge and center comes out clean. Serve warm with ice cream or whipped cream, if you like. Makes 6 servings.

CLASSIC APPLE PIE

rolled pastry for double-crust 9-inch pie
3/4 cup sugar
1/4 cup flour
1/2 teaspoon cinnamon
1/2 teaspoon nutmeg
dash salt
6 cups Granny Smith apples, peeled, cored, and thinly sliced
(about 6 medium apples)
2 tablespoons butter or margarine
milk for glaze

Heat oven to 425° F. Place bottom crust in deep 9-inch pie pan. In a bowl, mix together sugar, flour, cinnamon, nutmeg, and salt; stir in apples until thoroughly coated. Arrange apples in bottom crust; dot with butter or margarine. Cut slits in top crust and place over apples; seal and flute edges. Brush top crust with milk for a shiny glaze. Place on a small cookie sheet to catch any drips and bake 45 to 50 minutes or until bubbly. (To prevent crust edges from over-browning, cover edges with strips of foil until last 15 minutes of baking.) Cool before slicing. Makes 8 servings.

Classic Apple Pie

Indian Pudding

Apple Crisp

APPLE CRISP

4 medium Granny Smith apples, peeled, cored, and sliced

2/3 cup firmly packed brown sugar

1/2 cup flour

1/2 cup uncooked oatmeal

1/2 teaspoon cinnamon

1/2 teaspoon nutmeg

1/3 cup butter or margarine, softened

Heat oven to 375° F. Grease an 8" x 8" baking pan; place apples in pan. In a bowl, mix remaining ingredients thoroughly; sprinkle evenly over apples. Bake 30 minutes. Makes 6 servings.

CHERRY-NUT LOAF

2 cups flour

1 1/2 teaspoons baking powder

1/2 teaspoon salt

1/2 teaspoon baking soda

1 cup sugar

1/3 cup vegetable oil

2 eggs

1 cup milk

1 teaspoon vanilla

1/2 cup chopped maraschino cherries (reserve juice)

1/2 cup chopped walnuts or pecans

GLAZE:

1/2 cup powdered sugar

2 tablespoons cherry juice

2 tablespoons lemon juice

Heat oven to 350° F. Grease and flour 9" x 5" loaf pan; set aside. In a large bowl, stir together flour, baking powder, salt, and baking soda. In another bowl, beat together sugar, oil, and eggs until light; stir in milk and vanilla. Stir wet ingredients into dry just enough to moisten; fold in cherries and nuts. Spoon into pan, smooth top and bake 60 to 70 minutes, or until a toothpick inserted in the center comes out clean.

Meanwhile, make the glaze: Mix together powdered sugar, cherry juice, and lemon juice. While cake is still hot, pierce the top a number of times with a long, thin skewer, then pour glaze mixture over loaf. Let stand in pan 15 minutes, then turn out onto cooling rack. When cool, wrap well and leave overnight before slicing. Makes 10 to 12 servings.

Cherry-Nut Loaf

HONEY-PECAN STICKY BUNS

SYRUP:
1/4 cup butter or margarine
1/2 cup firmly packed brown sugar
2 tablespoons honey
1/2 cup chopped pecans

FILLING:
1/4 cup sugar
2 teaspoons cinnamon
2 tablespoons butter or margarine, softened

ROLLS:
1 package active dry yeast
1/4 cup warm water (105° to 115° F)
3/4 cups buttermilk or plain yogurt, warmed
1 egg
3 cups flour
1/4 cup butter or margarine, softened
1/4 cup sugar
1 teaspoon baking powder
1 teaspoon salt

To make syrup, melt 1/4 cup butter or margarine in a small pan; stir in brown sugar, honey, and pecans. Spread in a 9" x 13" pan; set aside.

To make filling, mix together sugar and cinnamon in a small bowl; set aside sugar mixture and butter or margarine.

To make rolls, dissolve yeast in warm water in a large mixer bowl; add buttermilk or yogurt, egg, 1 cup flour, butter or margarine, sugar, baking powder, and salt; blend with electric mixer 2 minutes, scraping bowl with spatula occasionally. Stir in enough remaining flour to make a soft dough that is slightly sticky. (You may have to use a wooden spoon at the end.) Turn dough onto a floured board and knead 5 minutes. Roll dough into a 9" x 15" rectangle. Spread dough with 2 tablespoons butter or margarine reserved from filling, then sprinkle with reserved sugar/cinnamon mixture. Roll up from the long side; pinch edges to seal. Cut into 1-inch slices. (An easy way to cut dough is to slide a length of heavy thread under the roll, then cross the thread on the top of the roll and pull it across so the thread cuts through.)

Place the slices on the pecan mixture in the pan. Cover lightly and let rise until doubled, about 40 minutes. Meanwhile, heat oven to 375° F. Uncover buns and bake 25 to 30 minutes. Immediately turn pan upside down on large tray and leave pan over rolls for a minute or two to let syrup drip. Remove pan and serve warm or cool. Makes 15 rolls.

BAKED APPLES WITH HONEY AND RAISINS

6 baking apples
3/4 cup granulated or brown sugar
1/2 cup raisins
1 teaspoon cinnamon
2 tablespoons butter or margarine

Heat oven to 375° F. Core apples and peel off top half of skin. Place in a shallow baking dish; set aside. In a bowl, stir together sugar, raisins, and cinnamon. Divide sugar mixture evenly among apples, filling the core of each, and sprinkle any remaining filling around apples. Dot each apple with 1 teaspoon butter or margarine. Add water to a depth of 1/4 inch. Bake 30 minutes, or until apples are tender; cool slightly before serving. Makes 6 servings.

Baked Apples with Honey and Nuts

Honey-Pecan Sticky Buns

SCRUMPTIOUS CARROT CAKE TO MAKE AND FREEZE

3 cups vegetable oil

8 eggs

4 cups sugar

1 tablespoon vanilla

4 cups flour

2 tablespoons cinnamon

1 tablespoon baking powder

2 teaspoons baking soda

1 teaspoon nutmeg

1 teaspoon salt

5 cups finely grated carrots

2 cans crushed pineapple (8 ounces each), well drained

3 cups chopped walnuts or pecans

Heat oven to 350° F. Grease and flour one of the following combinations of pans: two 9-inch springform pans, two 10-inch tube or bundt pans, four 4 1/2" x 8 1/2" loaf pans, or four 8-inch round cake pans; set aside.

In a very large mixing bowl, beat together oil and eggs with an electric mixer until light. Beat in sugar, 1/2 cup at a time, and vanilla. In another bowl, stir together flour, cinnamon, baking powder, baking soda, nutmeg, and salt. On low speed, mix flour mixture into sugar mixture just until blended. With a wooden spoon, fold in carrots, pineapple, and nuts. Divide batter evenly among prepared pans. Bake springform pans 60 to 70 minutes; tube pans 50 to 60 minutes; loaf pans 40 to 50 minutes; and cake pans 30 to 35 minutes, or until a toothpick inserted in the center comes out clean. Let cakes cool 15 minutes before turning out onto cooling racks. Cool completely before wrapping well and labeling for freezing. Can be frozen for up to 4 months.

To thaw, let stand at room temperature, wrapped, for 2 to 3 hours. Frost with buttercream or cream cheese frosting before serving, if you like. Whole recipe makes about 32 servings.

Scrumptious Carrot Cake

CHAPTER FOUR

WINTER COMFORTS

When winter arrives, good times are ahead—skiing, sledding, and building snowmen. Getting children in and out of snowsuits, hats, mittens, and boots is a kind of winter sport in itself. Winter also brings long, cozy nights near the fireplace and happy holidays filled with family, friends, baking, shopping, and gift giving.

For people who love to cook, winter can also bring an overwhelming desire to go into the kitchen and fill the house with the enticing smells of long-simmering stews or pot roast. When the mood strikes, cook up a Sunday Pot Roast (any day of the week) or Sausage and White Bean Casserole. Or try Stuffed Pork Chops, another very tasty, hearty dish that is quick to assemble, then takes care of itself as it simmers. Served with Garlic Mashed Potatoes and a green vegetable, the pork chops can be the center of a special family meal or dinner party with little work for the cook.

Making fruitcakes is an activity that can get children and other family members involved. Plan on making them the day after Thanksgiving so they'll be "ripe" for Christmas giving. Tart Fruitcake is perfect for those who find fruitcake that contains candied fruit too sweet. It's loaded with dried fruit, raisins, and nuts and keeps well for months. Once it's cut, though, expect it to disappear fast.

Mid-February can be a bleak time weather-wise, but it also presents a chance to show affection to extended family and neighbors by baking a Valentine's Day Chocolate Cake and sharing it with those you care about. Have loved ones over for a slice one evening during the week of Valentine's Day, or wrap it up and take it to work to share with co-workers.

As winter progresses and the post-holiday doldrums set in, create your own little celebrations to perk things up. Invite friends over for My Heart Cookies and coffee on a Sunday afternoon, or take a hamper of sandwiches and a thermos of Ice Skater's Hot Mulled Cider for a day of skating. By making pockets of fun through the season, you'll enjoy the winter and the good, warm food that goes along with it.

SALADS, STARTERS, AND SOUPS

AVOCADO AND GRAPEFRUIT SALAD

DRESSING:
1/2 cup olive or vegetable oil
2 tablespoons cider vinegar
2 tablespoons lemon juice
2 tablespoons honey
1 teaspoon Dijon mustard
1/2 teaspoon salt

SALAD:
1 large bunch watercress
2 grapefruits
4 ripe avocados

Mix all dressing ingredients in a jar with a screw-top lid; shake well. Arrange watercress leaves on eight cold salad plates. Peel the grapefruit and cut it into sections; divide the grapefruit evenly among the plates. Peel the avocados, slice lengthwise, and remove pits. Cut each avocado half crosswise into thin slices. As you finish cutting an avocado half, scoop it up with your knife and move it onto a plate, then press lightly to separate slices. Shake dressing again and pour some onto each salad; pass remaining dressing. Makes 8 servings.

WINTER GREENS SALAD WITH MUSTARD-ORANGE DRESSING

DRESSING:
1/2 cup mayonnaise
1/4 cup olive or vegetable oil
1/4 cup orange juice
2 tablespoons lemon juice
1 tablespoon Dijon mustard
1 teaspoon finely grated orange zest
1/2 teaspoon salt

SALAD:
2 cups romaine leaves torn into bite-size pieces
2 cups young spinach leaves torn into bite-size pieces
2 cups watercress or arugula leaves
1 head endive, cut crosswise into 1/4-inch slices

Mix all dressing ingredients in a jar with a screw-top lid; shake well. In a large salad bowl, toss salad ingredients. Just before serving, shake dressing again and pour enough over greens to coat lightly. Pass remaining dressing. Makes 8 to 10 servings.

Avocado and Grapefruit Salad

Warming Green Pea Soup

In a large, heavy pot melt butter or margarine and sauté onions and carrots until onion is golden; add ham and sauté 3 minutes. Add 3 quarts water, split peas, and rosemary; cover and simmer 1 hour, stirring occasionally. Stir in lemon juice and salt; taste and adjust seasonings. Serve hot with a sprinkling of pepper. Makes 8 to 10 servings.

WHITE BEAN SOUP

1 pound dried white beans of any variety
2 yellow onions, peeled and chopped
3 carrots, peeled and chopped
3 stalks celery, chopped
2 cloves garlic, peeled and minced
2 sprigs parsley
1/2 teaspoon dried oregano
1/2 teaspoon dried thyme
1/2 teaspoon red hot pepper sauce
1 tablespoon salt
freshly ground black pepper

Place beans in a large, heavy pot and cover with water; place over medium heat and bring to a boil; drain and cover again with water; boil and drain once more. Add 1 gallon water and remaining ingredients except salt and pepper. Cover and simmer about 1 1/2 hours or until beans are very soft; remove parsley sprigs. With a potato masher, partially mash beans and vegetables to make soup creamy. Add salt and pepper; taste and adjust seasonings. Heat thoroughly before serving. Makes 10 to 12 servings.

WARMING GREEN PEA SOUP

2 tablespoons butter or margarine
2 yellow onions, peeled and chopped
1 carrot, peeled and chopped
2 cups chopped cooked ham
1 pound green split peas
1 teaspoon dried rosemary
2 tablespoons lemon juice
1 tablespoon salt
freshly ground black pepper

White Bean Soup

CHICKEN STOCK TO MAKE AND FREEZE

5 pounds chicken backs and wings
1 yellow onion, quartered
1 stalk celery
1 carrot
1 bay leaf
6 peppercorns
2 thin slices lemon

In a large pot, cover chicken with 3 quarts water, then add onion, celery, carrot, bay leaf, pepper-corns, and lemon slices. Cover and simmer (do not boil) 1 hour. Allow to cool slightly, strain and discard solids. Refrigerate until fat rises then skim fat from top; reserve or discard fat. If stock has jelled, melt over low heat, then pour into 3 one-quart size zip-top freezer bags and label. Place bags flat in freezer until solid, then move them to a convenient area of freezer. Use in soups, rice, sauces, gravies, or stews. Makes about 2 1/2 quarts.

FRIED CHEESE STICKS

1 pound mozzarella cheese
flour
1 egg beaten with 1 tablespoon water
seasoned or plain fine, dry breadcrumbs
vegetable oil for frying

Cut cheese into sticks about 2 inches long and 1/2 inch square. Put flour on a plate, egg in a shal-low bowl, and breadcrumbs on a second plate. Roll each stick in flour, then in egg, then coat thor-oughly with breadcrumbs, patting crumbs so they stick to cheese. Let sticks rest on a rack while oil heats. Heat at least 1 inch oil to just below smoking point, then deep-fry sticks until golden. Drain on paper towels, then serve hot with a honey-mustard or barbecue dip, if you like. Makes about 10 servings.

BAKED CHICKEN NUGGETS

3 tablespoons vegetable oil
3 tablespoons butter or margarine
1/2 cup flour
2 tablespoons grated Parmesan cheese
1 teaspoon garlic powder
1 teaspoon paprika
1/4 teaspoon pepper
3 pounds chicken breasts, skinned, boned, and cut into 1-inch cubes

Heat oven to 400° F. Place oil and butter or margarine in a 9" x 13" baking pan and put in oven to heat. Meanwhile, in a paper or plastic bag, shake together flour, cheese, garlic powder, paprika, and pepper. Put a few chicken cubes at a time in the bag and shake to coat thoroughly. Roll each chick-en cube in the hot oil/butter mixture in the pan; bake uncovered for 25 minutes or until chicken is no longer pink inside and crust is brown. Serve hot with ketchup, chili sauce, or warm spaghetti sauce for dipping, if you like. Makes about 10 servings.

Chicken Stock

MAIN DISHES

MACARONI WITH HAM AND SPINACH

1 (10-ounce) package frozen
chopped spinach, thawed

3 tablespoons butter

1 small yellow onion, peeled and minced

1 clove garlic, peeled and minced

1 tablespoon flour

1 cup milk

1 cup ricotta or dry-curd cottage cheese

1/4 cup grated Parmesan cheese

1 cup diced cooked ham

1/2 pound elbow macaroni or rigatini,
cooked and drained

Heat oven to 350° F. Grease a 2-quart baking dish; set aside. Squeeze as much water as possible from spinach; set aside. In a medium pan, melt butter and sauté onion and garlic until onion is golden; stir in flour and cook until bubbly. Add milk and stir until beginning to simmer. Stir in ricotta cheese, 2 tablespoons of Parmesan, spinach, ham, and macaroni. Pour mixture into baking dish, sprinkle with remaining 2 tablespoons Parmesan and bake 30 minutes or until golden on top and bubbly around edges. Makes 6 servings.

Macaroni with Ham and Spinach

SPICY DUCK WITH BEANS AND GREENS

2 oven-ready ducklings (5 pounds each)
3 cups chicken stock
3 tablespoons butter
2 yellow onions, peeled and chopped
2 cloves garlic, peeled and minced
1 (10-ounce) package frozen chopped spinach, thawed
2 cans white kidney beans (15 ounces each),
drained and rinsed
1/4 teaspoon nutmeg
1/4 teaspoon pepper

Heat oven to 450° F. Remove fat from ducks' cavities and discard. Rinse ducks and pat dry; prick skin all over with sharp fork and place on a roasting rack in a roasting pan and roast, uncovered, 30 minutes, pricking and turning often to let fat drip off. Drain off fat from roasting pan, pour 1 cup chicken stock over ducks, reduce oven to 350° F, and roast 1 hour longer, basting frequently with pan drippings.

Meanwhile, melt butter in a large skillet and sauté onions and garlic until tender. Stir in spinach, beans, nutmeg, pepper, and remaining 2 cups chicken stock. Cover and simmer 20 minutes; remove from heat; taste and adjust seasoning, set aside, and keep warm.

Remove ducks from oven when done and cut into quarters. Divide spinach mixture into shallow soup bowls and top each with a piece of duck. Makes 8 servings.

SWEET AND SOUR MEATBALLS

2 pounds ground beef
2/3 cup fine cracker crumbs or matzoh meal
1/2 medium onion, peeled and minced
1 egg
1 1/2 teaspoons salt
1/2 teaspoon ginger
1/4 cup milk
1 tablespoon butter
2 tablespoons cornstarch

Spicy Duck with Beans and Greens

1/2 cup firmly packed brown sugar
1 (12-ounce) can crushed pineapple,
drained and juice reserved
1/3 cup cider vinegar
1 tablespoon soy sauce
1/2 cup chopped green pepper
1/2 cup chopped scallions, including some green tops

In a bowl, mix ground beef, crumbs, onion, egg, salt, ginger, and milk. Shape into bite-size meatballs. Melt butter in large skillet and cook meatballs, turning frequently. Meanwhile, in another bowl, stir together cornstarch, sugar, reserved pineapple juice, vinegar, and soy sauce. Remove meatballs and pour grease from skillet. Pour cornstarch mixture into skillet and stir constantly over medium heat until thickened. Let simmer 1 minute. Add meatballs, pineapple, green pepper, and scallions; heat thoroughly. Serve with rice. Makes 6 to 8 servings.

Sweet and Sour Meatballs

CLASSIC CHICKEN POT PIES TO MAKE AND FREEZE

1/4 cup butter

1/3 cup flour

2 cups chicken stock

1 cup milk

1 teaspoon salt

1/2 teaspoon paprika

1/2 teaspoon ground thyme

4 cups diced cooked chicken or turkey

2 packages frozen mixed vegetables
(10 ounces each), cooked and drained

2 cans or jars small whole onions
(8 ounces each), drained

1 (4-ounce) jar chopped pimiento, drained

pastry for 9-inch double-crust pie

milk for glaze

Lightly grease two 9" x 9" disposable aluminum pans; set aside. In a large pot, melt butter; blend in flour and cook, stirring, until bubbly. Add chicken stock, milk, salt, paprika, and thyme; stir constantly until thickened. Stir in chicken or turkey, vegetables, onions, and pimiento; cover and set aside while you prepare pastry.

Cut pastry in half and roll out each piece into a 10-inch square. Divide chicken mixture between pans, then fit pastry onto top of chicken mixture, turning under any excess at edges. Make slits in pastry, then brush lightly with milk. Wrap well for freezing and label. Place on bottom of freezer until frozen solid, then move to a convenient area of freezer. Freeze up to 3 months.

To bake, unwrap and allow to thaw at room temperature 1 hour, then place on a baking sheet and bake at 350° F for 1 hour or until crust is golden and edges are bubbly. Each pie makes 4 to 6 servings.

Classic Chicken Pot Pie

MEATBALLS STROGANOFF

2 pounds ground beef

2/3 cup fine cracker crumbs or matzoh meal

1 egg

1 1/2 teaspoons salt

1/4 teaspoon pepper

1/4 cup milk

4 tablespoons butter

1 medium yellow onion, peeled and chopped

2 tablespoons flour

1 cup beef stock

1 teaspoon Dijon mustard

1/2 cup frozen green peas, thawed

1/3 cup sour cream

In a bowl, mix ground beef, crumbs, egg, salt, pepper, and milk. Shape into bite-size meatballs. Melt butter in large skillet and sauté onion until until transparent. Add meatballs and cook thoroughly, turning frequently. Remove meatballs and onion; add flour to fat in skillet and stir until bubbly. Mix in stock and cook, stirring, until thickened; stir in mustard. Return meatballs and onion to skillet and stir in peas; cover and let simmer 3 minutes. Remove from heat and stir in sour cream. Serve with rice or noodles. Makes 6 to 8 servings.

SAUSAGE AND WHITE BEAN CASSEROLE

2 tablespoons olive oil

1 1/2 pounds kielbasa sausage, cut into 1/4-inch rounds

2 medium yellow onions, peeled and chopped

2 cloves garlic, peeled and minced

1 teaspoon dried oregano, crushed

1 teaspoon salt

1/2 teaspoon fennel seeds, crushed

1 cup tomato sauce

1 (6-ounce) can tomato paste

1/2 cup chopped parsley

2 cans white kidney beans (15 ounces each), drained and rinsed

Heat oven to 350° F. Heat oil in large skillet; add sausage and brown on both sides. Add onions and garlic to sausage and sauté 5 minutes or until onions are golden. Mix in oregano, salt, fennel, tomato sauce, tomato paste, and parsley; stir well. Add beans and stir. Pour into a 3-quart baking dish and bake, uncovered, 1 hour; stir occasionally. Makes 6 servings.

Meatballs Stroganoff

Turkey and Sweet Potato Pot Pie

TURKEY AND SWEET POTATO PIE

1/4 cup butter

1 medium yellow onion, peeled and chopped

1/3 cup flour

1 cup milk

2 cups chicken stock

1 tablespoon chopped parsley

1/2 teaspoon dried rosemary, crushed

1/2 teaspoon ground sage

1 teaspoon salt

3 cups bite-size pieces cooked turkey

2 cups bite-size pieces cooked or canned sweet potatoes

2 cups cooked green peas or green beans

12 biscuits

Heat oven to 425° F. Lightly grease a shallow 2 1/2-quart baking dish. In a large skillet or pan, melt butter and sauté onion until transparent; add flour and stir until bubbly. Add milk, stock, parsley, rosemary, sage, and salt; stir until thickened; let simmer 5 minutes. Add turkey, potatoes, and peas or beans. Pour into baking dish and arrange biscuits on top. Bake 30 to 40 minutes or until bubbly and biscuits are golden. Makes 6 to 8 servings.

Sunday Pot Roast

SUNDAY POT ROAST

3 tablespoons beef or bacon drippings or vegetable oil

1 5-pound boneless beef roast, such as rump, chuck, or bottom round

1 large yellow onion, peeled and chopped

2 bay leaves

3 cups beef stock

6 tablespoons flour

2 teaspoons salt

1/4 teaspoon pepper

Heat fat in a dutch oven and brown beef well on all sides. When beef is nearly finished browning, add onion and let it brown well. Add 1/4 cup water and bay leaves to dutch oven, cover tightly, and simmer over very low heat 3 hours, turning meat occasionally. Check often and add a tablespoon or two of water as needed. Remove meat to a platter and keep warm.

Pour drippings from dutch oven and skim off all but 2 tablespoons fat; discard bay leaves. Return 2 tablespoons fat, juices, and 1 cup beef stock to pan; over medium heat, scrape brown bits from pan. Gradually stir remaining beef stock into flour, then slowly pour into pan, stirring constantly, and cook until thickened. Reduce heat, cover, and simmer 3 minutes. Taste and adjust seasonings. Slice roast and serve with gravy. Makes 6 servings.

STUFFED PORK CHOPS

1 tablespoon butter

1 small yellow onion, peeled and finely chopped

1/3 cup finely chopped celery

1 tablespoon vegetable oil

1 cup seasoned dry bread cubes

6 rib pork chops, each 1 1/2 inch thick, with pocket cut in side of each

In a small skillet, melt butter and sauté onion and celery until soft; stir in oil and bread cubes. (If stuffing seems dry, sprinkle with water.) With a spoon, fill each pork chop with stuffing. Brush a large skillet with oil, then over medium-high heat, brown chops well on both sides. Cover skillet, reduce heat to low, and cook 45 minutes or until done. Makes 6 servings.

COUNTRY CAPTAIN CHICKEN

2 chickens (2 1/2-pounds each), cut into pieces

1/4 cup vegetable oil

2 large yellow onions, peeled and chopped

2 green peppers, chopped

2 cloves garlic, minced

1/3 cup chopped parsley

1 cup currants or raisins

1 tablespoon curry powder

1/2 teaspoon cayenne pepper

1/2 teaspoon dried thyme

1/4 teaspoon ground cloves

2 teaspoons salt

2 cans chopped tomatoes (1 pound, 12 ounces each)

2 cups chicken broth

3 cups hot cooked rice

1 cup toasted slivered almonds

In a large, heavy pot brown chicken pieces in hot oil; remove and set aside. In same pan, in remaining oil, sauté onions, peppers, and garlic about 8 minutes or until onion begins to color. Stir in parsley, currants or raisins, curry powder, cayenne, thyme, cloves, salt, tomatoes, and broth; return chicken to pan and simmer (do not boil) 30 to 40 minutes or until chicken is cooked through. Serve over rice, topped with almonds. Makes 6 to 8 servings.

Stuffed Pork Chops

SIDE DISHES

ROASTED VEGETABLE MEDLEY

1 sweet potato, peeled and cut into cubes
1 medium yellow onion, peeled and cut into eighths
2 carrots, peeled and cut into 1-inch lengths
1 green bell pepper, cut into strips
1 red bell pepper, cut into strips
1/2 teaspoon salt
1 tablespoon olive oil
2 teaspoons lemon juice
12 to 16 cherry tomatoes, stems removed

Heat oven to 425° F. In a 9" x 13" pan, mix sweet potato, onion, carrots, green pepper, and red pepper; sprinkle with salt, oil, and lemon juice; toss to mix well. Bake, uncovered, 25 minutes, then add tomatoes and bake another 10 minutes. Allow to cool to room temperature, then serve with any meat. Makes 6 to 8 servings.

BREAD STUFFING FOR CHICKEN OR TURKEY

1/2 cup butter
1 medium yellow onion, peeled and chopped
2 stalks celery, chopped
1/4 cup chicken stock or water
1/4 cup chopped parsley
1 1/2 teaspoons salt
1/2 teaspoon pepper
1 tablespoon fresh sage, minced
1 tablespoon fresh thyme, minced
8 cups soft raisin bread cubes

In a large skillet, melt butter and sauté onion and celery until tender; stir in stock or water, parsley, salt, pepper, sage, and thyme. Put bread cubes in a large bowl; pour wet ingredients over bread and toss to mix thoroughly. Makes stuffing for a 10-pound turkey or three 4-pound roasting chickens.

Bread Stuffing for Turkey or Chicken

**Warm Muffins
for Breakfast**

WARM BREAKFAST MUFFINS

1 egg

1 cup milk

1/4 cup vegetable oil

1 cup fruit: peeled, chopped apple, chopped cranberries,
or a combination

2 cups flour

1/4 cup sugar

1 tablespoon baking powder

1 teaspoon salt

Heat oven to 400° F. Grease 12 muffin cups. In a bowl, beat egg and stir in milk, oil, and fruit. In another bowl, stir together flour, sugar, baking powder, and salt; add to milk mixture and stir just until moistened—batter should be lumpy. Fill muffin cups 2/3 full and bake 20 to 25 minutes or until golden. Makes 12 muffins.

ICE SKATER'S HOT MULLED CIDER

3 quarts apple cider

1 quart white grape or cranberry juice

1/2 cup fresh lemon juice

1 cup firmly packed light brown sugar

1 orange

3 cinnamon sticks

12 whole cloves

In a large non-aluminum pan, heat cider, grape or cranberry juice, lemon juice, and sugar until sugar melts. Meanwhile, cut zest from orange in one long piece; tie orange peel, cinnamon, and cloves in a cheesecloth square; drop into cider mixture and let simmer 10 to 15 minutes. Discard spice bag. Makes 1 gallon.

Ice Skater's Hot Mulled Cider

MINNESOTA WILD RICE WITH GREEN PEPPERS

1 cup wild rice
3 cups chicken stock
1 teaspoon salt
1/4 cup chopped green pepper
2 tablespoons minced onion
1 tablespoon chopped parsley
2 tablespoons butter

Wash rice in a strainer under cold water. Place rice in a heavy pan with stock, salt, green pepper, onion, and parsley. Cover and bring to a boil, then uncover and cook gently, without stirring, about 45 minutes or until tender but not soft. Set heat to lowest and shake pan until rice is dry—about 5 minutes. Stir in butter and serve. Makes 6 servings.

MASHED GARLIC POTATOES

2 pounds all-purpose potatoes, peeled and quartered
1 teaspoon salt
1 tablespoon butter or margarine
4 cloves garlic, halved
1 cup buttermilk, warmed

Put potatoes and salt in a pan; add enough water to cover potatoes, and cook until tender—about 15 minutes. Meanwhile, in a small skillet, melt butter or margarine and over low heat, sauté garlic until very soft but not brown. Drain potatoes, leaving a few tablespoons cooking liquid in pan; mash with a potato masher or a fork. Fold garlic and buttermilk into potatoes. Makes 6 to 8 servings.

Minnesota Wild Rice with Green Peppers

QUICK HOLIDAY GIFTS

Dill Vinegar
Wash a large branch of dill and place into a decorative bottle, then pour red or white wine vinegar over it. Stop the bottle with a cork, then drip hot candle wax over the cork to seal. Label and tie a ribbon around the neck of the bottle.

Popcorn Tree
Make your favorite popcorn balls, wrap them in red and green plastic wrap or cellophane, and tie each with a ribbon. Tie the balls to a tree branch.

Cocktail Nuts
Heat about 2 inches of peanut oil to just below the smoking point in a large skillet or deep fryer. Fry raw almonds 1 cup at a time until pale golden, then remove to drain on paper towels. While still hot, sprinkle with garlic salt. When cool, transfer to decorative jars, then tie with a plaid ribbon.

Breakfast Basket
If you made jam during the summer, pack a jar into a large, napkin-lined basket along with home-made muffins, flavored butter in a crock, a couple of cheerful mugs, and a pound of special coffee.

DESSERTS

DRIED FRUIT COMPOTE

1 pound dried fruit (combination of prunes, apricots, figs,
raisins, peaches, and/or pears)
orange juice or water
1 stick cinnamon
1 thick slice lemon

In a stainless steel or ceramic pan, cover dried fruit with orange juice or water; add cinnamon stick and lemon slice. Bring to a boil, reduce heat, and simmer until fruit is tender and liquid is dark. Liquid will thicken slightly as it cools, or, if you like, remove the fruit and boil down the liquid until syrupy; return fruit to syrup and cool. Serve with vanilla pudding, ice cream, or yogurt, or serve over pancakes or crêpes. Makes 4 cups.

VALENTINE'S DAY CHOCOLATE CAKE

CAKE:
1/2 cup butter or margarine, softened
1 cup sugar
2 eggs
2 ounces unsweetened chocolate, melted and cooled
1 teaspoon vanilla
1/2 cup flour
3/4 cup chopped walnuts or pecans

FROSTING:
1/2 ounce unsweetened chocolate, melted and cooled
2 teaspoons butter or margarine, softened
1 cup powdered sugar
1 tablespoon milk
1 teaspoon vanilla

Heat oven to 325° F. Grease and flour an 8-inch round cake pan or a heart-shaped cake pan; set aside. In a large bowl, cream together butter or margarine and sugar; add eggs and beat well. Gradually blend in chocolate, vanilla, and flour. Stir in nuts. Spoon and spread in pan. Bake 30 to 35 minutes (do not overbake). Cool in pan 10 minutes, then invert on rack and cool completely.

While cake cools, make the frosting: In a medium bowl, stir together chocolate and butter or margarine. Add sugar, milk, and vanilla; beat until smooth. Spread on cooled cake. Makes 10 to 12 servings.

Dried Fruit Compote

My Heart Cookies

MY HEART COOKIES

1 cup butter or margarine, softened
1 cup powdered sugar
1 tablespoon cider vinegar
2 teaspoons ginger
1 teaspoon cinnamon
1/2 teaspoon nutmeg
3/4 teaspoon baking soda
1/4 teaspoon salt
2 1/4 cups flour

Heat oven to 400° F. Cream butter or margarine with sugar and vinegar. Blend in remaining ingredients and knead until smooth. On a lightly floured board, roll dough out 1/8 inch thick and cut with a heart-shaped cookie cutter. Reroll and continue cutting to use all dough. Bake on ungreased cookie sheets 8 minutes. Let cool 1 minute, then remove from cookie sheet and let cool on racks. Makes about 4 dozen cookies.

CHOCOLATE SPICE BUNDT CAKE

1 1/2 cups unsalted butter, softened
3 cups sugar
2 teaspoons vanilla
5 eggs
2 cups flour
1 cup cocoa
2 teaspoons cinnamon
1/2 teaspoon nutmeg
1/2 teaspoon baking powder
1/2 teaspoon salt
1 cup buttermilk
1 cup mini chocolate chips
powdered sugar

Heat oven to 325° F. Grease and flour a 10-inch tube or bundt pan; set aside. In a large bowl, cream together butter and sugar; beat on high speed for 5 minutes; add vanilla. Add eggs, one at a time, beating well after each addition. In another bowl, stir together flour, cocoa, cinnamon, nutmeg, baking powder, and salt. Add flour mixture to butter mixture alternately with buttermilk and 1/4 cup water, beginning and ending with flour. Fold in chocolate chips. Pour into pan and bake 60 to 70 minutes or until a toothpick inserted in the center comes out clean. Let cool 20 minutes in pan, then turn out onto rack to cool completely. Dust top with powdered sugar before serving. Makes 12 to 16 servings.

Chocolate Spice Bundt Cake

TART FRUITCAKE

4 cups flour
2 teaspoons cinnamon
1 1/2 teaspoons salt
1 teaspoon nutmeg
1/2 teaspoon baking powder
2 cups coarsely chopped pecans
2 cups coarsely chopped walnuts
2 cups chopped dried apricots
2 cups chopped dried pineapple
2 cups golden raisins
1 cup butter, softened
2 1/4 cups sugar
6 eggs
3 tablespoons brandy or whiskey
additional brandy or whiskey
for maturing cake

Heat oven to 275° F. Grease a 10-inch tube or bundt pan or two 9" x 5" loaf pans; set aside. In a very large bowl, mix together flour, cinnamon, salt, nutmeg, and baking powder; add nuts and fruit; toss together until well distributed; set aside. In another bowl, cream butter until light; add sugar gradually and beat until light and fluffy. Add eggs, one at a time, beating thoroughly after each addition. Blend in brandy or whiskey. Pour the batter into the flour mixture and fold only until well combined. Pour into pan(s) and bake 2 1/2 hours or until just beginning to pull away from sides of pan.

As soon as cake comes out of oven, sprinkle it well with additional brandy or whiskey. When liquid has soaked in, turn cake out of pan and cool completely on a rack. Wrap well in waxed paper, then in foil. If you like, unwrap and sprinkle with additional liquor every few days, but stop at least 1 week before cake is to be eaten. Store at room temperature for up to 3 months. Makes about 24 servings.

GEORGE WASHINGTON'S CHERRY CAKE

3 cups flour
1 teaspoon cinnamon
1/2 teaspoon ground allspice
1/4 teaspoon salt
1 cup buttermilk
1 teaspoon baking soda
2 cups sugar
1 cup butter or margarine, softened
5 eggs
1 cup cherry preserves, chopped

Heat oven to 350° F. Grease and flour two 9-inch round cake pans. Sift together flour, cinnamon, allspice, and salt; set aside. In a small bowl, mix together buttermilk and baking soda (it will fizz); set aside. In a large bowl, cream sugar and butter or margarine until light and fluffy. Add eggs, one at a time, beating well after each addition. Add buttermilk and flour mixtures alternately (beginning and ending with flour) to the butter mixture. Add preserves and stir well. Pour into prepared pans and bake 40 minutes, or until the edges begin to pull away from the pans and a toothpick inserted in the center comes out clean. Cool 10 minutes in pans; invert onto cooling racks and cool completely. Frost with White Icing (page 32) or buttercream frosting, if desired. Makes 8 to 10 servings.

CREAMY RICE PUDDING

1/2 cup uncooked short-grain white rice
3 cups milk
1 cup heavy cream
2 eggs
1/4 cup sugar
1/8 teaspoon salt
1 teaspoon vanilla
nutmeg
2 tablespoons butter or margarine

In a pan, bring rice and 1 cup milk to a boil; cover, reduce heat to low, and simmer 12 minutes or until most of milk is absorbed; set aside. Heat oven to 350° F. In a bowl, mix together remaining milk, cream, eggs, sugar, salt, and vanilla; stir in cooked rice. Pour into a shallow 1 1/2-quart baking dish, sprinkle with nutmeg, and dot with butter or margarine; place baking dish in a larger pan and pour 1 inch of hot water into outside pan. Bake 1 1/2 hours, stirring occasionally, until creamy. Serve warm or chilled. Makes 6 to 8 servings.

INDEX